KingdomNomics

Enjoy a Life That Will Echo into Eternity

by Phil Wiegand

"He is no fool

who gives what he cannot keep

to gain that which he cannot lose."

Jim Elliot

CONTENTS

ACKNOWLEDGEMENTS

F irst, I wish to thank my lovely wife, Ruth Ann, because she has encouraged me to write this book for a long time. Years of studying the Bible from a business perspective have given us some unique spiritual insights and applications that we wished to share with our family and as many other people as possible. Her loving counsel and advice over the years have been invaluable.

Secondly, I wish to acknowledge Helmut Teichert, who was the catalyst for bringing this book project to fruition. As the project manager, he helped focus the message, established a basic structure for organizing the material, and recruited and led the team that made this book a reality.

I am particularly thankful that Rob Suggs was willing to take on this writing project. As a professional writer and accomplished wordsmith, Rob waded through my many pages of notes and masterfully transformed them into a manuscript. His professional style of writing and composition have made this book what it is, an easy and very meaningful read.

I also want to acknowledge Sheryl Moon for her wonderful and skillful efforts in editing these pages to make sure that all the editorial issues were properly addressed.

I am so grateful to my team for making this book possible.

KingdomNomics

IS A DISCIPLINE COMMITTED TO
EXPERIENCING MAXIMUM RETURNS
IN LIFE AND ETERNITY.

1

Life's Leading Indicators

L et's step around the corner of time, shall we? Let's pay a visit to the next phase of your life.

Why not? I have some ideas about the possibilities of everyday living. I've tried and experienced them myself, and I've seen them lived out by people I care about.

I can predict what might be in store for you. As a matter of fact, I've made much of my living in the prediction business. I examine a stock, make an educated projection about its future, and invest accordingly. I've learned that the future of any stock is all about the people who stand behind it. So I've had to learn about people, too. I've had to observe their values and their habits.

> *KingdomNomics is the study of the principles defining value from God's point of view.*

In both kinds of ventures—in the fates of stocks and people—there are what we call "leading indicators" that predict future performance. We look to certain factors to help us predict success.

This book is all about the leading indicators of *your* life. These leading indicators consist of a set of principles I've come to group under the title of *KingdomNomics*—the organization of economics under the laws of God's kingdom.

KingdomNomics is more than theory. It's a discipline committed to experiencing maximum returns in life and eternity. We all have time, talent, and treasure, and these are being consumed daily. The question is, by what? Are they being consumed for the sake of temporary pursuits, or toward things that are eternal?

I think of daily time like daily bread. Each one of us has a "loaf" of time, if you will. Each day consumes one slice, and the loaf becomes smaller as time passes. We eventually realize this, to our dismay, and it becomes so very important to expend our given time wisely—to make our lives count for something meaningful.

> *Our focus is not on today's easy pleasure; it's on eternal significance.*

That's what KingdomNomics is all about: knowing and experiencing the benefits of joyfully trading earthly, temporary gratification for something that will last forever.

KingdomNomics is living life by the principles defining value from God's point of view, as outlined in the Scriptures. We apply these principles in the decisions that determine how we invest our time, our talent, and our treasure, the "three Ts" of kingdom advancement. For those who take seriously the coming of a new life—one that follows earthly life—nothing could be more important.

And yet so many of us live as if these decisions are trivial, expending those three Ts with little thought of the fact that what we do here echoes into eternity. The kingdom thinker, however, develops an *I want to make a difference* attitude, looking at the important matters and seemingly trivial ones alike and thinking, *How can I do something for the kingdom here? Something that will last?*

Then he discovers something truly thrilling: worldly wealth comes and goes, but he, acting on kingdom principles, can become rich in the world to come by making the right investments in this one. He *can* take it with him—if it's the right "it." That means focusing on what matters to God, and we do that by the application of *KingdomNomics*.

But before we simply jump in and start making decisions, it's important to understand two key truths that provide the foundation for all of the principles related to *KingdomNomics*:

1) *KingdomNomics* requires a different set of priorities, and
2) *KingdomNomics* requires that we have only God as our ruler.

THE ROAD LESS TRAVELED

The first truth is reflected in what Jesus said about salvation:

> *Enter through the narrow gate. For wide is the gate and broad is the road that leads to destruction, and many enter through it. But small is the gate and narrow the road that leads to life, and only a few find it.*
>
> Matthew 7:13–14

Jesus is saying that many people choose what is easy. Few people champion the kind of principles we're discussing here. Fewer still are those who will live them out. Being intentional about the use of our time, talent, and treasure is difficult. So we may not be surrounded by a great crowd of enthusiastic adherents to these ideas. But they are still true. They actually work in this life, bringing great joy and contentment.

The real question is this: "Am I going to aspire to be one of the few strategic Christians[1] in this world who lives out the incredible truths of *KingdomNomics*, rather than simply talking about them … or will I take the easy way that leads to unprofitable results?" Will you look back from the vantage point of eternity and know you've pursued the right things, or will you have made poor choices?

It's true that *KingdomNomics* principles have incredible benefits *here and now*—but they also require discipline, wisdom, and sacrifice. We live in an instant gratification world in which people want easy fixes and simple solutions. If this were a book that played to those impulses, it would easily find a large audience. But our focus is not on today's easy pleasure; it's on eternal significance. Our ultimate joy is deferred to that "someday" life. Each of us must choose what matters most.

Every day I see people living out the well-known parable of Jesus, in which various people are entrusted with certain sums of money (see Matthew 25:14-30). Some people simply hide their resources. Some consume every dollar they have, as well as dollars they don't have (leading them into debt). Others invest a little, yet still consume more than necessary. Still others earn incredible dividends by investing wisely and sacrificially. From a purely financial perspective, disciplined investment is wise. However, from a kingdom perspective, the implications are exponentially profound. It is the path of the narrow road.

We have mentioned leading indicators of a kingdom-based life. Perhaps the most important of all is your check-book. What does it reveal about you? If you were to study its columns of entries, would you find most of those entries pointing to things that pass away, or things that endure forever?

Paul said of kingdom-based people that "we fix our eyes not on what is seen, but on what is unseen, since what is seen is temporary, but what is unseen is eternal" (2 Corinthians 4:18). The idea is so simple, yet so challenging. I have to ask myself from time to time, "Does my checkbook truly

> *The human heart has room for only one ruler. Which ruler have you chosen?*

reflect that I have my eyes fixed on the unseen and eternal things that are important to God?"

That's the leading indicator of my heart and soul. It demonstrates what matters to me, regardless of what I *say* matters. I know that *KingdomNomics* dictates that my checkbook speaks of a life consumed by eternal realities.

So our first truth is that we will have very different priorities from most people. Unless we keep our eyes focused on God, we will tend to drift back toward the ways of the multitude.

THE RULE OF ONE

Secondly, Jesus makes this challenging statement about the investment of life:

No one can serve two masters. Either you will hate the one and love the other, or you will be devoted to the one and despise the other. You cannot serve both God and money.

Luke 16:13

The challenge here is that *KingdomNomics* requires incredible focus. We will serve money, or it will serve us ... as we serve God. It's an all-or-nothing proposition, because the human heart has room for only one ruler. Which ruler have you chosen?

You lose nothing and gain everything by choosing God. Most people choose money for the love of "things." But in the New Testament, Paul tells Timothy that God "richly provides us with everything for our enjoyment" (1 Timothy 6:17). When you choose God, "things" are much less of a problem. But if you choose money, you could possibly lose the blessing of God forever. As a matter of fact, you could fall into the traps of greed and excessive consumerism, finding you never have enough!

Remember another statement Jesus made:

But seek first his kingdom and his right-eousness, and all these things will be given to you as well.

Matthew 6:33

C.S. Lewis, a twentieth-century writer, put that verse in his own words: "Aim at heaven and you will get earth thrown in. Aim at earth and you get neither." [2]

That's a pretty strong statement. If you give your life to God—all of it, unreserved—you are aiming for heaven.

And then you are amazed by what is "thrown in." Sure, your path may still take you over some major bumps in the road. But you find yourself happier and more energetic than you've ever felt.

You have deeper love, for God and for people. You have stronger hope in everything—even the current state of our world—because you know it's all in God's hands. You feel a true peace, because you understand this truth: *You are no less than God's investment capital in his creation.* He invested *you* in this world, and you're here to make a difference for him. He put you here to bear fruit (John 15:5).

> *Will you be consumed by the temporary and unsatisfying things of this world, or with the passion of living for Christ?*

When you make your life an investment for the kingdom, you feel the deepest joy there is. How do I know this? I am experiencing it! It's the reason I feel a deep calling to share what I've learned through this book. There's nothing more important to me than helping others to learn the liberating truths that God has for us through *KingdomNomics*.

For the first thirty years of my life, I had no conception of such things. In a chapter to come, I'll tell you a little about my journey and how I finally came to the truth that turned me around in my tracks.

But first, we'll discuss the three kinds of lives that we see believers following today. You're likely to be surprised by what we'll reveal about our common assumptions about God and money.

Then we'll visit some key principles of *KingdomNomics*. I try to use simple illustrations, as well as a few life stories, to keep things clear and relatable.

In the end, of course, what matters most is that God speaks to you and shows you that your life *will* be invested, one way or another. It all comes down to your time, your talents, and your treasure, and how you use them. These are the most important decisions you'll make. Will you be consumed by the temporary and unsatisfying things of this world, or with the passion of living for Christ?

I pray that the answer will be as clear for you as it's been for me.

KingdomNomics

IS SEEING OURSELVES AS GOD'S STEWARDS
FOR THE STRATEGIC USE OF RESOURCES—
GREAT AND SMALL.

2

THREE KINDS OF BELIEVERS

L et's begin by breaking down your life to the lowest common denominators.

We'll start with *God*–the One who made you.

Then there is *you*.

Then there are your *resources*—everything you can use or interact with in this world, including time, talent, and treasure.

So we have three entities. And we can think about each one of these entities as being a circle. The questions are: How do they relate to one another? Do they overlap, or does each one stand alone? And if they overlap, which circle takes precedence? How do you relate them to one another? You relate to God and to your resources, but do those circles relate to each other?

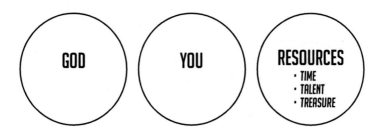

Do you approach your resources based on your beliefs about God? Or do you approach God based on your resource needs? Or do those two circles never even intersect, having nothing to do with each other?

As we discussed in the last chapter, Jesus said that one of these "circles" will actually become the master of the other—you will serve God *or* money. It's clear, then, that how you relate to these questions will make a far-reaching statement about who you are, how you live, and who you are becoming.

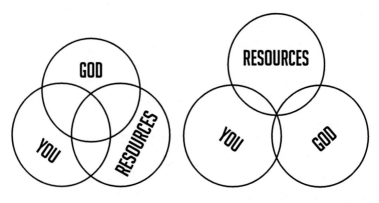

I'm something of a student of human behavior, including my own. I've watched my family, my friends, and my acquaintances. I've read biographies of other people. And I've come to some conclusions about how most people in the world relate to God and his gifts. With regard to those who do make some kind of attempt to serve God, I've come to the conclusion that there are basically three kinds of believers in this world and they are defined by how they relate to the God-circle and the resources-circle.

1. EARTHLY-MINDED BELIEVERS

The first category of believers I've identified is a large one, perhaps because it requires the least thought. It's the "default" position, the one most under the influence of basic human nature.

These individuals accept what God has given them and use their resources for their own comfort, pleasure, and personal gratification. In other words, these people see the God-circle and the resources-circle as separate spheres that very rarely overlap.

For example, when it comes to the stewardship of treasure, studies indicate that while Americans give $40 billion annually to churches, they spend the same amount on their pets. Very few Christians give one tenth of their income to church or spiritual causes. Do a large number of believers "put something in the plate?" Of course. Do they do so under the guidance of deeply considered Christian thinking? That's another question. Meanwhile, half or more of our church members rarely or never give at all.[3]

The Earthly-minded Believer sees money the way nearly everyone else does. He wants to keep as much of it as possible, and use it for his own personal enjoyment of life.

There's nothing wrong with enjoying the financial fruits of our labor. God wants us to do so. The important question is this: Are you spending completely on things that pass away like a vapor—or are you investing significantly in the things of God that will last forever?

The biggest danger to this category of people is that Earthly-minded Believers usually have no idea what is happening to them. Materialism is so seductive! People believe they're simply living the good life and pursuing the

American Dream. They may be attending church, studying the Bible, and following Christ in many ways. But they've compartmentalized the sphere of all of their resources, whether time, talent, or treasure. They haven't brought these under the Lordship of Christ. Their resources-circle is not intersecting with their God-circle. "Their mind is set on earthly things" (Philippians 3:19).

Needless to say, we need to be spiritually alert and far more perceptive about eternal matters as they touch earthly ones.

2. CHRISTIAN PHILANTHROPISTS

The next category of believers is one that gives more attention to giving.

These are believers who have come to the conviction that God has blessed them, and they should give back a portion of what they've received to help support ministry and missions. For them, this is somewhat of a duty, an obligation to fulfill, like paying taxes or voting.

There's an "oughtness" that guides them. They write a check or volunteer in some way, but there is no joy or purpose in it. Perhaps it's the way they were taught by their parents. Perhaps it is motivated by the sense of duty of "chipping in" so that the church can fund some project overseas, or pay its budget, or provide some program. Perhaps it's giving out of guilt. The important distinction is that it is "doing what I have to." As a result, it's not something

> *We need to be spiritually alert and far more perceptive about eternal matters as they touch earthly ones.*

particularly pleasant or enjoyable. Just like paying taxes, it's seen as a necessary requirement.

Again, to provide an example related specifically to treasure, George Barna's research tells us that the average Christian gives no more than 2 percent of his income to the church or other ministries. [4] What does that suggest to us? It tells us that people are giving as little as possible, and they are giving without joy.

As we'll see later, sums of money aren't important. What we're discussing here is the attitude in the mind of the giver, and we know that when people love doing something, they do it more frequently. If people show great hesitancy to do something, then we know it brings them little or no satisfaction.

Giving of treasure in the New Testament, particularly in the book of Acts, is something that happens as a natural, spontaneous overflow of the spiritual adventure. People are so thrilled to see what God is doing, and to be a part of it, that they give all that they have to support what is happening. No one talks about "percentages," because they're so busy talking about the greatness of what the Spirit of God is doing.

Paul, however, presents another approach to giving when he addresses the Corinthians. This approach is what we might call proportional giving:

> *Now about the collection for the Lord's people: Do what I told the Galatian churches to do. On the first day of every week, each one of you should set aside a sum of money in keeping with your income,*

> *saving it up, so that when I come no collec-*
> *tions will have to be made.*
>
> 1 Corinthians 16:1–2

"In keeping with your income" is a common-sense measurement that tells us that each person should give as he or she is able. We give proportionally.

We also see in this passage that Paul is telling people to be diligent about giving in preparation for the time when the funding is needed. This is the principle of intentionality. But it's always an act of joy and participation with God—there are never set requirements or limits.

In *KingdomNomics*, we ask ourselves over and over: Are we seeing ourselves as God's stewards for the strategic use of resources, great and small? Or are we giving haphazardly, without thought or plan, or out of some sense of legalistic obligation? Where is the sense of gratitude and joy?

Some Christian Philanthropists actually do enjoy their giving, in a certain sense. It is sacrificial, but they wear their sacrifice as a kind of badge of honor. "I gave until it hurt." Sometimes we do give in a deeply sacrificial way, but what we're after is giving until we feel not hurt, but a deep sense of fulfillment, in partnering with the eternal work of God.

3. KINGDOM INVESTORS

There is one other kind of believer and, as you might predict, this one is harder to find among us.

The Kingdom Investors are people who grow in Christ, who dig deeply into his Word, and who come to see their resources in a brand new way. Never again will they look upon their assets as mere money or mere things, but as part and parcel of what God is doing in this world and through their lives. They bring the circle marked "resources" into the greater, all-defining circle marked "God."

Kingdom Investors see all that they have and all that they own as their sacred trust, theirs to use strategically for the advancement of Christ and his eternal purposes. Their time, talent and treasure is no longer an end in itself, but a medium, a palette to be used in the beautiful art of serving God.

Are we seeing ourselves as God's stewards for the strategic use of resources, great and small? Or are we giving haphazardly, without thought or plan, out of some sense of legalistic obligation?

Who are these people? You'll find them across the spectrum, from those who have a great deal of money, to those who don't have much at all. From those who have a great deal of time to share, to those who can only give a little. And those who have a great deal of talent, to those who only have a little. Some of these believers are led to invest in missions on the far side of the globe; others give themselves to the work of God just down the block. Many diversify, insisting on having a hand in God's work in every place possible. They follow their hearts, finding joy and exhilaration in the specific areas and needs where the Holy Spirit leads them.

The Kingdom Investors deploy whatever time, talent, and treasure they have available, and it's a pleasing truth that while not everyone can invest great sums of financial wealth, everyone can give their time and their personal talents. These are all things that God has given so that we might find the unique joy of giving them back.

We've all heard of the 80/20 rule. In most churches, it's probably true that 80 percent of the giving and 80 percent of the hands-on ministry is done by 20 percent of the people. But even fewer are those who truly discover the *KingdomNomics* principle of the all-out maximizing of our resources for God's kingdom.

Jesus talks about a man who finds a treasure buried in a field. This man goes out and sells everything he has in order to raise funds to buy that field. He believes he has nothing that isn't expendable toward gaining the precious treasure he has glimpsed. (See Matthew 13:44.) That's how it is for the Kingdom Investor. He has caught a glimpse of a treasure nothing on earth can match—an eternal treasure. All that he has must be invested toward that treasure.

> *Kingdom Investors see all that they have and all that they own as their sacred trust, theirs to use strategically for the advancement of Christ and his eternal purposes.*

Jesus also told stories about masters who gave their servants sums to invest. The workers were held accountable not for using their resources and not for preserving them, but for *multiplying* them. (See Matthew 25 and Luke 19.) The master, of course, is Christ. And why does he take time to give us sums to invest? His work is the work we were made to do! Christ wants us to know the unique thrill of bearing fruit in his name; taking what he has given us, and giving it back in multiplied amounts.

Kingdom Investors live in this world but see into the eternal one: "Since, then, you have been raised with Christ, set your hearts on things above, where Christ is, seated at the right hand of God. Set your minds on things above, not on earthly things" (Colossians 3:1–2).

Does that lessen their caring about the here and now? No, it's just the opposite. Their eternal values give them a deeper concern for others: "Not looking to your own interests but each of you to the interests of the others" (Philippians 2:4). And they seek "the good of others" (1 Corinthians 10:24).

Kingdom Investors are also motivated by the rewards that the Bible promises. The New Testament often speaks of rewards given to believers in heaven, based upon the right kind of behavior in this life. Jesus often said that hypocrites and those with empty religion have already received their rewards. It is constantly taught that those who obey Christ can look forward to wonderful things in eternity.

MORE ABOUT KINGDOM INVESTING

The heart of the Kingdom Investor is quite different from the one motivated simply by guilt or sense of obligation. Kingdom Investors have found their treasure—their pearl of great price. It's not as if they throw away all that they have to pursue it; they actually *use* all that they have to enhance it.

That's the adventure of this life. Kingdom Investors see it as a matter of sowing and reaping, which is a simple principle that is true in every aspect of life in this world:

> *Remember this: Whoever sows sparingly will also reap sparingly, and whoever sows generously will also reap generously. Each of you should give what you*

have decided in your heart to give, not reluctantly or under compulsion, for God loves a cheerful giver. And God is able to bless you abundantly, so that in all things at all times, having all that you need, you will abound in every good work.

2 Corinthians 9:6–8

The Kingdom Investor, of course, wants to reap generously. He knows that God loves a cheerful giver, but he's a cheerful giver because he knows God. Why have only a little fulfillment, a little satisfaction? He wants as much of it as possible, because no other joy on earth can match the joy he feels when he knows the kingdom of God is being served.

The Kingdom Investor also begins to experience the favor of God in his life, which is a reward of service. The life of generous giving is a life that God blesses. Have you ever met a truly godly giver who is unhappy? Again, the Kingdom Investor says to himself, *I must have more of this! I must know God even more deeply. I must multiply my time, my talents, and my treasures even more so that I can serve him better.*

Kingdom Investors live in this world but see into the eternal one.

And never is there a thought of comparing his giving to that of others. Never does he seek personal credit for what he does, because those things are not the source of the joy. When God is glorified, that's when the Kingdom Investor is energized. That's when he receives his reward. "We do not dare to classify or compare ourselves with some who commend themselves. When they measure themselves by themselves and compare themselves with themselves, they are not wise" (2 Corinthians 10:12).

KingdomNomics teaches us that kingdom investing is a privilege, a pleasure, and a deep reward on many fronts, in this world as well as the world to come.

There are those in this world who know and understand the financial markets, at least from a worldly point of view, and they are making money. Others dabble in the markets, not truly comprehending how they work, so that they lose what they have. But whether they make or lose fortunes, none will find real meaning in life until they discover the ultimate goal of investment. Resources are the tools God has given us to get us involved in the great story of what he is doing. Purposed for this world alone, time is simply a commodity, talent is often used for personal recognition, and money is mere paper or fine metal. But when invested for God's purposes, it can be so much more—it can be a touchstone to the eternal world.

KingdomNomics

BEGINS WITH A GENUINE RELATIONSHIP
WITH JESUS CHRIST.

3

THE GREED FACTOR

"Phil, could you come in for a minute?"

I'd heard the door of the study open, and my father wanted to have a talk with me. Had I gotten into some kind of trouble? No, my father wanted to teach me something about the world.

I sat across from him as he produced an impressive sheet of paper and placed it in my hands. "Phil," he said, "this is what we call a stock certificate. It's very, very important."

He went on to explain that as long as he held this document, he had proof that he owned something: some piece, or "share," of a business concern that was engaged in the earning of money. Whenever that company made new dollars, he would get his share, paid out in "dividends."

This was all new information for me, but I could already see how powerful the concepts were. I could earn money by going outside, mowing the lawn, and getting paid for it—or I could pay someone to give me a percentage of what they earned when *they* did it. I could buy into the work of others.

When my father saw I understood that much, he said, "There's more, son. And this is where it gets exciting.

When you receive your dividends—your earnings—what do you do with them?"

I thought I had the right answer. "Put it all in the bank? Save them?"

"Not exactly. You have to buy groceries, right? And pay your bills. So you do that with some of the money. Then, you take the rest of it and look for more shares to buy."

"Oh—and that's how you could get rich!" I was seeing the light.

"Yes, Phil, if you're smart about how you do it. You will generate a stream of income that continues to grow larger. Sort of like running a dairy farm."

"What?"

He laughed, and took back the stock certificate. "Let's say for a minute that this is the deed to a cow. It produces milk, and you sell the milk, right? With the proceeds of that milk, you buy another cow. This one produces milk, too, and now you have *two* streams of revenue. You never sell the cows—until they grow old and stop producing. Healthy cows are your money-makers. You sell the milk and buy more cows."

> *Deep down, I realized that accumulation had changed me on the inside, and I didn't like how.*

I looked back at the certificate, and he said, "Whether it's milk or oil or cars—anything people can produce and sell—you want to keep buying these shares of their business. They give you leverage to buy still more shares. So, if you get a bad cow occasionally, that's all right, because you have other cows to cover the loss."

This talk changed the way I viewed the world. I thought about lots of cows giving lots of milk, and making lots of money. Why, everyone could be rich!

No, that wasn't exactly right. Only buying the right cows, my father explained, would make that possible. So education was critical when it came to equipping myself to enter a highly competitive world of people with the same dreams of cows, cash, property, and natural gas wells. I would have to do my best in the classroom to get the edge, so I could start earning wealth as soon as possible. That wealth would generate greater wealth.

That was the extent of my thinking. I wanted to make money. Why? To make more money. Why? The theme of my life was mostly thinking about the accumulation of wealth. I thought that was the American Dream. Because when you have enough money, you can do what you want, when you want.

And it was working, too. I discovered that my father had told it to me straight. The cow theory of investing was as effective as it was simple, and I was on my way to becoming a prosperous man.

ON THE INSIDE

I learned other lessons, too—some of them unexpected and unwanted.

I had wondered what happened if the farmer simply kept buying cows. Wouldn't he end up stuck with too much milk to sell?

Ordinarily, it seems logical. But an economist from the 1800s, J. B. Say, put forward a different theory. Say's Law basically said that supply creates its own demand.

Build it and they will come. We know it works out that way in our economy: Active buying and selling creates more buying and selling, new markets, and that's good for overall business.

But is it necessarily good for *us* if that is our only concern? And by *us*, I mean who we are, deep inside.

Here's a law no one has named: Increase the supply of money, and it will change *you*. Yes, build it, and they will come. But just who or what will come? Greed, lust, and every form of desire. Deep down, I realized that accumulation had changed me on the inside, and I didn't like how. I had perceived myself working in a vacuum, happily growing wealthier on the outside while remaining the same old Phil within. But I had changed.

None of us believe that the desire for "more" will overpower us, but it happens every time. You simply don't hear many people say, "I've made more money than I can ever spend. Now I'm going to enjoy it." No, they seem to work even harder. They make even greater investments. Millions aren't enough—they want billions. And they lack any semblance of contentment.

The Bible, as if peeking into the twenty-first century, nails it:

> *Whoever loves money never has enough; whoever loves wealth is never satisfied with their income. This too is meaning-less. As goods increase, so do those who consume them. And what benefit are they to the owners except to feast their eyes on them?*

Ecclesiastes 5:10–11

Note that it's not whoever *has* money; it's whoever *loves* money. Love is reserved for God and his children, not things. Also note that Say's Law is reiterated in verse 11. It's the *love* of money that is "a root of all kinds of evil," as Paul writes (1 Timothy 6:10). The real issue is: Can you keep a proper relationship with what you own?

Oh, you'll have the best of intentions. "I can handle it," you'll say. But greed and selfishness—which are among the roots that silently coil into the cellar of the wealthy person's life—will grow. It happened to me; I wanted to invest more and more money rather than simply what

> *Greed and selfishness— these are among the roots that silently coil into the cellar of the wealthy person's life.*

was ordinary or healthy. I saw myself as a consumer, but *I* was the one being quietly consumed.

We talked earlier about the *why* questions: *Why* more money? *Why* still more after that? There comes a time when these questions rise to the surface, when we look at ourselves and say, "What's the point of all this? Where does traveling the trail of *more* eventually lead? And what price am I paying to take that path?"

There are other questions too—questions about what's inside us; questions about the soul. Where is God in all this pursuit of more? What is it that *he* wants me to pursue? We have a spiritual instinct that tells us that we've wandered far from God when life becomes only a great quest for finance.

One night I turned on my TV set and saw Billy Graham speaking to a great crowd. I respected this man; I was curious about what he was saying. He was explaining that many experts on the Bible believed we were coming to the end of history, and that soon we would each have a personal reckoning with our Creator.

God uses precision timing. Certain words and messages come before us because we've arrived at the moment he has prepared for us to hear them. And I heard. It seemed

> *My appetite for God's Word became almost insatiable.*

as if Billy Graham was speaking to me personally. He was teaching me about the biggest issues of life just as surely as my father had taught me the economics of cows and cash.

He asked what would happen to my eternal soul if I were to die that evening. And I had no answer.

Maybe I wouldn't die that night. But it was going to happen, and it was probably going to be a surprise when it did, and as things stood, I wouldn't be ready. My heart was in disarray.

I struggled with what to do. My first instinct was to go to church. But my childhood impression of churchgoing was that when you went to church you put on a coat and tie, and I couldn't see what that had to do with anything today.

This was a crossroads moment. I came very close to making some weak excuse, and moving on with my life.

RETHINKING RESOURCES

However, something inside me wouldn't let me walk away and discard that confrontation with eternal truth. In the end I found a church, and there I heard about what it means to live as a true follower of Jesus Christ. It wasn't enough to for me to intellectually accept Christ's reality. I had to know him in a genuine relationship. I had to let him have all of me, so that every sin and imperfection within me could be cleansed in the way that only he could accomplish.

There wasn't anything I could do. I could only come before him in humility; but that was all right, because he *could* and *would* do the rest. He could cleanse me, forgive me, and make me a new creature.

I came to understand what it meant for Jesus to die on that cross—that he did it to pay the penalty for all that was wrong about me. A perfect man was punished so that a guilty one could go free: *me*.

And best of all—it was a gift! With my orientation in financial transactions, this was hard for me to believe. There was no dickering or bargaining here. All I had to offer was my flawed and broken heart, worthless to anyone but the One who created it; what I had to gain was deep joy, indescribable peace, and full forgiveness now—and eternal life later.

What wise investor would reject such a deal?

I prayed and asked Jesus to come into my life, trusting only in him and nothing else to make me right with him. And I meant it.

My first action was to find a bookstore and make two purchases: a modern translation of the Bible, and *Halley's Bible Handbook*, which helped to give me some idea of where to find what I needed in the pages of Scripture.

Taking a cue from Dr. Graham, I turned quickly to Revelation, the final book of the Bible. Much of it was hard to understand, but this much was clear: the world wasn't going to continue forever the way it was. God was going to bring history to a close, and I wanted to be spiritually ready for that.

I learned what it meant to pray daily, to share my faith, to enjoy Christian fellowship. But I was shocked to discover how much the Bible had to say about my money. I had always simply assumed that this was a book about matters of the soul.

Well, it was. But as it turns out, there is no dichotomy between what is in the heart and what is in the hand. The heart governs how we use our possessions, and, in turn, our use of possessions impacts the heart.

I now had to overhaul all my attitudes and beliefs about money, right down to the cow principle, and rethink all of my financial theory from a biblical perspective.

For example, Jesus said, "Watch out! Be on your guard against all kinds of greed; life does not consist in an abundance of possessions" (Luke 12:15). This verse forced me to see the first 30 years of my life for what they were. I would never have described it that way, but life for me had indeed been all about how much stuff I could accumulate.

> *I now had to overhaul all my attitudes and beliefs about money and rethink all of my financial theory from a biblical perspective.*

I didn't simply need to see money in a new light; I had no idea about the true meaning of life.

I knew now that I lacked wisdom. But that wasn't discouraging at all—it was energizing. I knew that, in Christ, all the news was good, even if it meant tearing down my old walls of self and building something new. Jesus loved me; he wanted what was best for me, and I was more excited and eager than I'd ever been. I had that hunger that new believers often have in which I couldn't get enough of

God's Word and I couldn't hear enough good teaching. My appetite for God's Word became almost insatiable.

What was money all about, if it wasn't simply about *more*? What was my goal, if it wasn't simply more cows and increased sales of milk?

I was getting the milk of the Word, and it tasted very good. I began to grow and to see the world through new eyes.

KingdomNomics

IS USING ALL OF OUR RESOURCES
TO GLORIFY GOD.

4

WHO'S THE BOSS?

As I moved deeper into a life of following Christ, I made an observation. There were a number of believers who were very casual about their faith. Perhaps they hadn't had the eye-opening experience of coming to grips with their own spiritual danger, as I had. I knew I had a real desperation to truly know God and to please him in all that I did, while some people weren't as eager to grow spiritually.

In my business dealings, I had found some Texan people to be colorful and entertaining. They had a saying about some people being "all hat and no cattle." (Cows—again!) I got their point. There are some people who can make a good appearance with nothing to back it up. I didn't want to be a Sunday pew cowboy—I wanted to be authentic.

So I thought about who I was and what God had given me to work with. Finances, of course, had been at the center of my life. What changes did God want to make in how I approached money? Should I just give it all to the missionaries? Put it in the bank and forget about it? Burn it with the backyard leaves?

I thought of another Texas saying, this one from Humble Oil. That forgotten company, from Humble, Texas, was the precursor to Exxon. Some of their execs used to say, a bit tongue-in-cheek, "We aren't very smart, but we have a lot of money." Again, that's just who I *didn't* want to be—a guy with a lot of dollars and no sense.

Jesus once said we should be "as shrewd as snakes and as innocent as doves" (Matthew 10:16). Actually, the Bible has plenty to say about being common-sense smart in everyday life. The book of Proverbs is packed with encouragement to handle money wisely. I had done that, for the most part. What needed to change was my attitude toward it.

> *Jesus says I must choose one master, and everything else must be in submission to that decision.*

I realized that I needed to begin seeing money in terms of God's kingdom. God hasn't given us time, talent, and treasure just so we can hoard it or spend it on ourselves. All of our resources can be used to glorify him. So where to start?

I kept coming back to that powerful command from Jesus, given in the Sermon on the Mount:

> *No one can serve two masters. Either you will hate the one and love the other, or you will be devoted to the one and despise the other. You cannot serve both God and money.*
>
> Matthew 6:24

That verse became a new foundation for me, and it is the foundation for this little book.

At first, the words seemed very cut and dried to me—as if one must choose to love or hate money, with no middle ground. It was a very difficult verse to understand, so I began to study it carefully. I learned what I could from sermons and Bible studies, and the truth began to come into focus for me.

When Jesus made this statement—and several others on the subject—he used the word *mammon* for what we translate here as money. This word means "all that one possesses apart from his body and his life." In other words, things—*stuff*, whether it's money or what it buys.

The word *mammon* also comes from a root word that means *entrust*. That's a serious, heightened version of trust. Similar to today, people of that time would give their money to a banker, and they had to place all their faith in that banker to take care of their worldly wealth. Jesus is saying that we can't fully *entrust* ourselves to both God and possessions. We can't divide it all up and invest 50/50.

But Jesus did a little more with this wor*d mammo*n. He could have simply talked about money in the way most people think of it: capital, coin, currency. Instead, he breathed life into the concept. He spoke of "serving" *mammon*, making *mammon* the name of a master who can lord it over his slave. In his day, of course, there was genuine slavery, and the word he used in this verse for *serve* was associated with that kind of servitude. So this is serious trust and serious service.

Ultimately, here is what Jesus meant: As a human being, you can't help but serve something or someone. You will serve God, or you will serve things and stuff. You'd better make that decision carefully, because one of these will win, and it will win all of you. You're entrusting no less than your heart and soul—your eternal destiny. Jesus says I must choose one master, and everything else must be in submission to that decision.

CHOOSE A LANE

Ultimately, I came to understand that Jesus was talking about *idolatry*. Idolatry? Well, that word makes us think about strange statues and exotic sacrifices. What could that have to do with money?

When Jesus talked about *mammon,* he was making the point that whether you realize it or not, you are in service. You may live under the illusion of total freedom, that you think what you want and do what you want, beholden to no one. But true freedom is indeed an illusion. You are always *pursuing*, or you wouldn't be a human being. Pursuing what? It could be money or comfort. It could be power or pleasure or acclaim. But something drives you, it drives you down its own road, and Jesus says that it's impossible to travel on two roads at the same time.

> *Since you and I were made to honor and serve God, we become idolaters when we honor and serve anything or anyone else.*

Since you and I were made to honor and serve God, we become idolaters when we honor and serve anything or anyone else. That's what I came to understand: I had clearly been walking down a certain road, and it was the endless road of pursuing *more*. But it ultimately had no real destination other than chasing a mirage ending in heartbreak. I wasn't enjoying the journey.

As I've said, it's a crossroads moment when we realize this. However, we can take a detour. It's a very hard and deliberate choice. Have you ever watched a driver undecidedly swerve from lane to lane before a fork in the road?

36

You want to shout, "Pick a lane!" You can't drive in two directions at one time.

That's what Jesus was saying. You have to determine which road to choose. You must decide who or what to pursue.

In the Bible, God's people once found themselves at this crossroads. They knew they were moving into a new land, and they were going to create a new life. Their leader, Joshua, challenged them to make their choice of whom to follow:

> *Choose for yourselves this day whom you will serve ... But as for me and my household, we will serve the LORD.*
>
> Joshua 24:15–16

Joshua was recognizing that the people of Israel, through all their travels, had collected a wide assortment of gods, all of whom were now competing for the hearts of the people. Some were the pagan gods of the days before the true God had revealed himself. Others were the gods of Egypt, where the people had been slaves. And still others were the gods of the present moment, in the place where the Israelites were camping.

They had served and were serving all these gods, because people are easily influenced. Rarely do we make hard and fast choices about what ultimately matters. We copy those around us, or do what we were raised to do.

Joshua called the people to be more alert than that—to know the choices, make one, and live with it. And he and his family were choosing to serve the Lord.

I wonder if you've ever had a Joshua moment, as I did. Have you ever stopped and realized that it was time to choose your own path, rather than to simply follow the crowd?

If we'll only stop and take a hard look, the choice isn't very difficult. A favorite verse of mine says, "Those who cling to worthless idols forfeit the grace that could be theirs" (Jonah 2:8, NIV84). You can look at the world around you and at history to see the fate of those who build their lives around the pursuit of worldly wealth. It's a cruel and merciless master that drives and drives, without ever giving satisfaction, without ever giving rest.

Yet Jesus says, "Come to me, all you who are weary and burdened, and I will give you rest" (Matthew 11:28). I never found true rest until I went back to that banker called *mammon*, withdrew everything, and deposited it within the Bank of Heaven.

I've chosen my road, I know where it leads, and I feel perfect peace about it.

CHOOSE YOUR WATER

Why does life work this way? Why must it be such a dichotomy? Why can't I neatly compartmentalize my life—like I do my luggage, for example—with a neat little compartment for spirituality, another for career, another for family and friends? Then I could pursue what I wanted when I wanted, as easily as reaching into the suitcase for a necktie.

The answer, I've found, is in the human heart and how it works. The heart is like a sponge that soaks up everything around it. When you squeeze the sponge, you'll get out exactly what you've let that sponge absorb. The sponge doesn't have neat compartments. It has a lot of empty space ready to be filled. The heart is the same way, and you decide how to fill it.

So if your heart soaks in the dirty water of bad ideas in this world, that's what fills it. You begin to think and feel accordingly. I spent three decades of my life taking in bad ideas about what constituted life, and I had to do a lot of squeezing to empty them out. I had to review the thoughts and assumptions and values that had guided me for all

I never found true rest until I went back to that banker called **Mammon,** *withdrew everything, and deposited it within the Bank of Heaven.*

of that time. Occasionally, I still have to battle vestiges of that former life.

Most of all, however, I needed to do some more sponging—in the right places. It was time to take in the pure and living water of the gospel. Jesus once came to a village where he met a woman drawing water at the local well. He knew every drop of the "dirty water" in her life, and he compared it to what he had to offer. Pointing to the well, he said,

> *"Everyone who drinks this water will be thirsty again, but whoever drinks the water I give them will never thirst. Indeed, the water I give them will become in them a spring of water welling up to eternal life."*
> John 4:13–14

That's what it means to stop following the wrong master and begin following the only one who will love you and give you all the joy and peace you've been longing for.

When I only pursued wealth, the deep thirst inside me was never quenched. No business deal, no new possession was ever enough. It was like drinking salt water; my thirst just became deeper.

The things of this world aren't designed to give lasting purpose and contentment. They never have and they never will. Serving *mammon* is trusting things and self rather than trusting the one who made them. It's handing over your precious life to an untrustworthy banker who doesn't want your prosperity and happiness, but your ruin.

> *The things of this world aren't designed to give lasting purpose and contentment.*

I use the sponge principle to help me remember that I must constantly be renewing and refreshing my soul with that living water; I must also be squeezing out the impurities that I'm sure to take in just by living in the world. Watching some things on television allows dirty water to enter. Being with certain people can do that. Even left to my own thoughts, I take in dirty water because I am a fallen, flawed human being. Jesus has forgiven me, but the "old me" is always hanging around. He wants his place back.

So by the power of God's Spirit, I soak in the truth found in God's Word. I spend time each day talking with Jesus in prayer. I pay attention to what kinds of people I listen to, what kinds of cultural influences I award with my attention.

One other fact about sponges: Have you ever seen what happens when an old sponge is put aside and left unused? It dries out. It becomes brittle. Once your heart belongs to Christ, you need to soak it in the living water daily. Salvation happens in a moment in time, and it can never be taken away from you.

What you *can* lose is the fresh joy of your walk with him, so don't let your spiritual vitality run dry. The more often that happens, the more you'll find it losing its natural absorbency, like the sponge. Spiritual growth must be a constant pursuit, a way of life. The good news is that there's nothing more delightful or encouraging. We'll say more about "soaking it all in" later, but for now, know this: It's your life's greatest joy.

KINGDOMNOMICS

IS SERVING GOD
AND GOD ALONE.

5

AIMING AT NEW TARGETS

As I thought about the God vs. *mammon* issue, I realized I had to topple the idols in my life. I had to start walking a new path, never looking back, never letting the "old me" make a comeback.

When I was in school, I took it for granted that there would be tests and examinations occasionally. That was the proving ground for whether I had really learned anything. I found now that God hands out a test every now and then, too. It's one thing to say, "I am going to devote my life wholeheartedly to God from now on. I will entrust everything to him." It's another thing to live that out in a moment of crisis.

> *Whatever controls your mind, whether it's God or money or something else,* **controls you.**

One of the big exams for me came when I was diagnosed with prostate cancer some years ago. Nowadays, we hear a lot about this health threat, but when I was diagnosed, many of the treatments were just being developed. I had no idea whether I had been handed a death sentence, or, if I did survive, whether there would be debilitating effects that would drastically change life as I had known it.

Because of the surgeon's schedule, it turned out that I would have a period of waiting for a particular nerve-sparing procedure that was then new and rare. And so the waiting began.

Have you ever had to wait for an ominous, frightening event? It tends to bring life into focus. It sorts out the trivial from the significant. God had my full attention during this time, if only because of the fear that came over me. I would love to tell you that I had the heart of a lion, but I got myself all worked up inside. I ended up aggravating an atrial fibrillation problem in my heart.

What a mess. I can remember telling my wife Ruth Ann that I wondered if I'd even make it to the surgery, and never mind the aftermath. She wanted so badly to comfort me, to encourage me, but fear had an icy grip on my spirit.

What I did have, of course, was my faith. I prayed, *What now, Lord? What should I do? What should I feel?*

I walked back to my study one day and had an honest heart-to-heart talk with God. I poured out my feelings, my questions, my pleas. And as I did so, I felt his presence in a genuine way. I had an urge to take a sheet of paper in hand and write the word *CHRIST* in large letters. And as I looked at that powerful name, I felt his comfort begin to flow through me. He promised us that he would walk with us even through the valley of the shadow of death.

A NEW VISION

The six letters in the name—CHRIST—began to suggest an acrostic to me. I opened up my Bible and wrote:

C is **COMPANIONSHIP**—"God has said, 'Never will I leave you; never will I forsake you.' So we may boldly say: "The Lord is my helper; I will not fear. What can man do to me?" (Hebrews 13:5-6).

I *knew* that nothing could separate me from him. Suddenly and physically, I felt an incredible flow of peace course through me as I wrote the words for that verse—a very clear physical feeling of a great burden of a spirit of oppression being lifted from my back. *Wow! What just happened?* I had to sit for a moment, catch my breath, and let it all sink in before I could take up the pen and write again. When I did, I wrote furiously, verses coming to me from years of teaching Bible classes and doing my own study:

H is **HOPE**—"Therefore, with minds that are alert and fully sober, set your hope on the grace to be brought to you when Jesus Christ is revealed at his coming" (1 Peter 1:13).

Now I had a *target* for hope: for him to be real to me in this situation. That meant so much!

R is **RECEIVE**—"Receive with meekness the implanted word, which is able to save your souls" (James 1:21, NKJV).

I realized I needed God's Word, which holds awesome power. It is living and powerful (Hebrews 4:12).

I is **I**—"I have been crucified with Christ and I no longer live, but Christ lives in me. The life I now live in the body, I live by faith in the Son of God, who loved me and gave himself for me" (Galatians 2:20).

This isn't the old me! I'm a new creature! Christ would live in me, empowering me to go through this experience.

S is **SUBMISSION**—"We take captive every thought to make it obedient to Christ" (2 Corinthians 10:5). "The mind governed by the Spirit is life and peace" (Romans 8:6).

I should set my thoughts on eternal things, letting the Spirit of God watch over them. This enabled me to reject fearful thoughts and replace them with his promises when fear raised its ugly head.

T is **TOTAL TRUST**—"Commit your way to the LORD; trust in him and he will do this ... Be still before the LORD and wait patiently for him" (Psalm 37:5–7).

In this verse I began to experience total trust. Being still and experiencing God's presence changed everything. He makes things happen.

It was very clear to me that God had prepared me for this moment; that he was now unpacking years of my study of the Word, and using it to empower me. I was too excited to sit. I leaped to my feet and ran to tell Ruth Ann all about it. We looked at each verse together, and we realized the impact this would have on our lives.

I had felt as if I'd been in a little boat stalled in the middle of the ocean, waiting for the hot sun and deep thirst to finish me off. I'd never felt more alone. But then the wind of the Holy Spirit filled my sail and brought me to safety. He provides the power to move us through life, and without him, we have no hope. I felt fresh and powerful encouragement.

Whatever controls your mind—whether it's God or money or something else—*controls you*. I made up my mind that for the rest of my life, nothing but the power of Jesus Christ would be the wind in my sails.

CHRIST OVER SELF

Once we begin to follow Christ seriously, all the targets change for us. We're walking that new road, and therefore we look for different landmarks. And as we are changed by the Holy Spirit, our goals change too.

The greatest target change of all, of course, is whom we live to please. In our human nature, we believe that life is all about self-help and self-emphasis; everything is *me* oriented. Advertisers build all their campaigns on the vanity and self-absorption of people in general. Next time you're in the grocery store, glance at the checkout aisle magazines. What articles are being pitched? I believe you'll find an assumption that those in the grocery line are self-absorbed. People drop out of churches or marriages simply because "this isn't meeting *my needs* anymore." And the world sees that as a perfectly justifiable point of view.

The choice to serve God and God alone means that we live to please him rather than ourselves. There's no way to overstate how great a leap in perspective that is. Our flawed, sinful human nature keeps pointing us toward the self-driven life at every turn: "Look out for number one!" "You have to toot your own horn." "You have to do what's best for you."

But Christ beckons to us, saying, "Whoever wants to be my disciple must deny themselves and take up their cross daily and follow me" (Luke 9:23).

That may not sound like the best marketing plan: *Deny yourself!* It might not go over well in the check-out line, but it's a message made by God for the human heart.

As it turns out, the way of self-absorption—attractive as it initially is—leads only to brokenness and despair, while the way of following Christ leads to deep joy and fulfillment. This is why Jesus said, in the very next verse following his statement about denying oneself, that "whoever

The greatest target change of all, of course, is whom we live to please.

wants to save their life will lose it, but whoever loses their life for me will save it" (Luke 9:24). You find yourself by giving yourself away.

I know—it takes a while to wrap your mind around that one. It's counterintuitive. It seems like a paradox. But I've found it to be true—the more you try to please yourself, the less you'll be pleased. The more you focus on Christ, the more pleasing life becomes.

The "Me First" life is a dead-end street.

FAITH OVER ACTION

Another target change is in *how* we live. The old target was performance, the new target is faith. For thirty years, I felt as if I needed to keep running, keep working long hours, keep chasing after worldly goals. Even after I became a Christian, some of those goals were simply replaced with other goals, more Christian but still performance-based.

This represents another very difficult paradigm for us to take in. All over the world, all through history, people have built their religions around action—earning the attention of the gods, earning forgiveness, earning blessings. Christianity is unique in that it says that, as good as good works are, they can't do a thing to earn us God's love or forgiveness. This comes from grace, through the work of Christ on the cross for our behalf. And then we please God through *faith*—a living relationship of trusting him.

A favorite verse of mine is this: "And without faith it is impossible to please God, because anyone who comes to him must believe that he exists and that he rewards those who earnestly seek him" (Hebrews 11:6).

Life before Christ is like hustling to serve a slave-master or a boss you can never please, a harsh taskmaster. Life in Christ is a relationship of love and friendship and grace and acceptance. As a result, you want to give, to serve, to do things for God and others—but out of the overflow of joy rather than a way to buy approval.

Years ago, a member of our board pointed me to a corporation that was important in his life. There were shares of this company's stock available at a certain price. I did my homework, liked what I saw, and called my friend on the phone to let him know I wanted to purchase the stock, if it was still available.

It was such a simple, ordinary chain of events that I couldn't have imagined the good things that would result. A long-term business and personal friendship began. Without my knowing or expecting it, my friend began to open doors to new companies and new relationships for me which provided me with new and expanded opportunities. I experienced something very rare and special in our business. I had shown interest in what mattered to him, and he wanted to respond in kind. It was a grace relationship.

My point is that I wasn't seeking his "blessings" to serve myself; I was simply doing what a good businessman would do. But it opened a relationship, a friendship, not just a cold business transaction. This is what God does when we show interest—as we do through faith—in the things that matter to him. He begins to bless us. He begins to open new doors of opportunity, new possibilities.

If we approached him selfishly, it wouldn't work this way. If we tried to earn his favor through service, it wouldn't work this way. Living by faith means we experience wonderful relief from living a performance-based life. God responds to the grateful heart. He is relational, and he loves to bless his faithful children. "All these blessings will come on you and accompany you if you obey the LORD your God" (Deuteronomy 28:2).

GIVING OVER TAKING

Another new target is that we stop looking for ways to *get* things out of life, and we become more interested in *giving* things. This is a guiding principle of *KingdomNomics*. We need to be "givers," not "takers." This, of course, is bound up in both of the previous two target changes. We want to please God instead of self; we want to please him with faith rather than works. And so our spirit begins to change; we become more interested in what pleases him, and we discover that what pleases him most is to help advance his kingdom. We can do this through giving—all kinds of giving.

The natural human tendency is to take. We don't see ourselves as selfish, or think of ourselves as takers. But our fallen human nature causes us to "look out for number one." And when we live in a world of countless people all looking out for themselves, all competing

> *Life in Christ is a relationship of love and friendship and grace and acceptance.*

for the same things, all wanting to take, then the world is full of conflict. It becomes an ugly place.

But what happens when people begin to see themselves as serving a common goal? What happens when we serve not ourselves, but Christ, and as a result, others? The world is transformed.

Jesus said, "It is more blessed to give than to receive" (Acts 20:35). The word *blessed* has the connotation of happy, of being favored in life. It's not just that *God* is pleased when we give; *we're* pleased, too. It's *fun* to be a giver.

What has meant more to you—receiving a nice Christmas present, or giving one that you really thought about and planned? God designed us to be givers, and once we find that out, we discover, *Wow! I had no idea that would feel so good.*

I've observed how the church often brings out that old Bible verse, "God loveth a cheerful giver" (2 Corinthians 9:7, KJV) every year during budget-pledging time. It seems as though the message is "Get out your wallet, and you'd better do it with a smile on your face."

That's not how it is at all! Doesn't God already own it all? Does he really *need* us to give? I believe that God doesn't really *need* us to give, he *desires* us to give, because of the *joy* it will bring us and the *work* it will do for his kingdom.

Living by faith means we experience wonderful relief from living a performance-based life.

Giving pleases God, and it pleases us, too. It sets into motion principles of kingdom giving, kingdom logistics, kingdom investment, and a whole world of joy that comes out of doing exactly what God created us to do.

In the next few chapters, we'll explore a little of that world. We'll discuss exactly what life becomes as we begin to apply the principles of *KingdomNomics* to our lives.

KingdomNomics

IS DEPENDENT UPON
THE HOLY SPIRIT'S POWER.

6

KINGDOM POWER

If you can understand and apply to your life the following sentence, then you'll be among the wisest and
best informed of Christians.

All of our spiritual power comes from the Holy Spirit.

Simple enough, right? And yet somehow, after two
thousand years of Christianity, a great many believers do
not understand this. As a matter of fact, they don't even
grasp who the Holy Spirit is! That's like having no idea
you have a heart pumping blood through your system, or
that your house is wired with electricity. The matter of your
power in the Spirit of God has incredible implications for
every day of your life.

The Holy Spirit is Christ living within us. He offers us
guidance and just the right words when we face various
crises. He comforts us. He strengthens us. He administers
the special gifts given to us for ministry. It is through him
that we live as new creations in Christ. On the day you
began to believe in Jesus, his Spirit took residence within
you. And he began the great work that will continue until
either you die or Christ returns to earth—the power of
transforming you into the living image of Christ.

And how does he do this? Over the years, I've developed an understanding of the process by which we are changed. I think of it this way: *We soak, we sow, and the Spirit flows.*

First comes *soaking* our hearts and minds in the Word of God. There's no substitute for this, no shortcut. We need to immerse ourselves in the Word of God until as much of it as possible is engraved on our hearts.

I hear some people say that they struggle to read and understand the Bible. There are a number of guides and study Bibles to help us do that, but what's important is that we must read the Bible itself—not just a good book, but *the* Good Book. The Holy Spirit within us reveals its truth. He interprets and he applies the message of God to our thoughts and our issues.

All of our spiritual power comes from the Holy Spirit.

If you've ever struggled to stick with Bible study, hang in there. Ask God to bring the words to life for you, as he has done for thousands of years. One of my all-time favorite verses is from the psalmist: "My heart is stirred by a noble theme as I recite my verses for the king; my tongue is the pen of a skillful writer" (Psalm 45:1). The composer of this verse had dipped his mind into the lovely depths of Scripture. Note that he "recited" his verses before the king. This means he had committed them to memory.

I can't count the many times my life has been blessed because of a verse I hid in my heart on some earlier occasion. Every verse you memorize gives the Spirit a ready tool to use just when you need it. Soon, he can do some major work on your insides!

The heart is stirred when we look deeply into Scripture and meditate on it. So much power is contained in these heaven-sent lines. Nothing expresses the great issues and principles of life the way the Word of God does.

The psalmist's heart is stirred as he *soaks* it in the Word. We've used the sponge as a word picture for this, with its absorbency, filling up with living water.

And then, as we read or recite our verses, we *sow* them to the Spirit, and he begins to *flow* through our being, so that we feel the power and presence of God. I've enjoyed this dynamic experience countless times. We come to the Word of God anxious, and he gives us peace. We come with anger about someone, and he gives us love and patience. We come dry, and he fills us to bursting with the refreshment of his goodness. It's a daily reality check with a sweet fragrance.

This is one of the primary ways that kingdom attitudes begin to grow within us. Crisis by crisis, worry by worry, relationship by relationship, the Spirit of God, speaking to us through his Word and his personal guidance, transforms us into the people he has always intended for us to be.

A genuine "spiritual chemical reaction" takes place when we soak our hearts and minds in the Scriptures, and let the Spirit flow freely through us. Life, health, power, and hope surge through us like medicine from heaven itself. This is one reason that so many studies show that people who pray are physically and emotionally healthier than those who do not. The life-giving power of God flows through those who pray and who recite their verses to the King.

So we *soak*, we *sow*—reciting our verses, and the Spirit *flows*. Soon, we'll need to repeat this process. The sponge (heart and mind) can be filled over and over, and we can't let it become dry and brittle. It's a repeat process. However, the more we do it, the more we find that our attitudes are changing in a remarkable way. It works the same as with any form of nutrition: You must eat daily, but eating the right foods begins to bring you a residual health. You are stronger and healthier.

THE MIXMASTER CONCEPT

I often explain the *soak*, *sow*, and *flow* process with the illustration of a Mixmaster and three steps in using it.

First, I drop the ingredients into the bowl to *soak*. I compare this to memorizing the living and powerful Word of God. It will work in the heart of the believer if he receives and trusts it as divine. It is sitting in your heart and mind, waiting for something to happen.

Second, the Mixmaster stirs the ingredients. I compare that to *sowing* to the Spirit. As we recite our verses, the Spirit stirs the Word, mixing himself with it, causing our hearts to be stirred with a noble theme as we focus our thoughts and eyes on Jesus Christ, the fountain of life.

Finally, the mixture is ready to be poured out. The Spirit *flows*, imparting his life into our mortal body. Now we can go into our day with Christ, the power of God "who is able to do immeasurably more than all we ask or imagine, according to his power that is at work within us" (Ephesians 3:20, NIV84).

Our worldview and our value system take on a whole new perspective. We become ambassadors for Christ, constantly engaged in calling people to be reconciled to him. My wife can see the difference in me when I emerge from a time of *soaking*. I can see the difference in her as she does it. There is a stronger contentment, a peace about the worries of the day, a confidence in the direction we're heading. And I find that I want to keep memorizing God's Word, so that it is a living, working presence in my heart, no matter where I am or what I'm doing.

Most of all, I gain a renewed sense of connection to the things that God cares about. I sow my verses to him, and I reap what I sow; he imparts truth and conviction and peace. I also fend off temptation and bad decisions more effectively. My life is radically different because of what happens when I soak in the Word, sow to the Spirit, and let the Spirit flow.

> *On the day you began to believe in Jesus, his Spirit took residence within you.*

Paul captures what this is all about when he writes, "May the God of hope fill you with all joy and peace as you trust in him, so that you may overflow with hope by the power of the Holy Spirit" (Romans 15:13).

FLOWBACK FROM THE SPIRIT

One of the simplest truths known to humanity is that we reap what we sow. *Flowback from the Spirit* is the phrase I use to describe what I reap when I sow to the Spirit by reciting God's Word. It is manifest in many different ways: the secrets that God imparts to us; "light bulb" moments when we suddenly and clearly see something God has been trying to tell us; specific areas of guidance; and simple gifts of encouragement, strength, and power just when we need them.

We're recalling and meditating upon the Word of God, affirming its truth, and in doing so, we're "putting on Christ" (see Galatians 3:27), setting the Spirit free to

have his way with us. I've made specific kingdom investments and other life decisions that I knew were the result
of flowback from the Spirit.

Perhaps my most vivid example of flowback in my life
was when I was in a serious automobile accident. It was
amazing enough that I even survived it. I totaled my jeep,
fractured my sternum, broke my tibia, and lacerated my
forehead with many tiny bits of glass.

In short order, I was in the intensive care unit of the
hospital, and I was discovering what physical pain was all
about. The doctors were
concerned about possible
fluid buildup around the
heart, due to my chest
injury. It hurt almost
beyond endurance if I coughed—which I kept needing to
do—or even moved. The doctors couldn't give me anything
for my pain other than simple acetaminophen, because my
heart had to be monitored.

*The process by which we
are changed: We soak, we
sow, and the Spirit flows.*

When they changed the sheets on the bed, they had
to lift me by a small crane because I lacked the power to
move myself. Yet with all that pain, it was for the best that I
wasn't "dosed up" with some strong medication. I was alert
enough to recite my verses to God. All my years of study
brought Scripture passages to mind, the most prominent
one being, "For the eyes of the LORD range throughout the
earth to strengthen those whose hearts are fully committed
to him" (2 Chronicles 16:9).

There's so much power in these words. I knew the
eyes of God were upon me, and I felt his strength even in
my terrible pain. But I concentrated on making sure my
heart was fully committed to him in that awful moment.

I sowed to the Spirit, and "my heart [was] stirred with a noble theme" (Psalm 45:1). No, the physical suffering did not go away, but the Spirit imparted contentment, peace, and (I believe) health to my physical body.

Being spared pain is fine; *triumphing* over pain is far more exciting, far more of an investment toward wisdom and strength in the Lord. That's what he was doing for me. He loved me enough to let me grow through that trial, and he was there with me every second.

A nurse smiled at me and said, "Someone must have really been watching over you during that accident."

One of the doctors said, "We've studied the accident report, and wonder how you did not die and managed to come through it without real damage to your heart. With auto accidents, most fractured sternums are vertical. The heart is punctured, and death is instantaneous. Yours was a lateral fracture. Tell me," said the doctor with a grin, "exactly what did you do to deserve surviving an accident like this one?"

"Nothing," I said. "I fully deserved to die on that dark road. But I was saved by the grace of God." And I prevailed through the worst of it by flowback from the Spirit, experiencing his incredible presence and encouragement and healing power fixing my thoughts on his Word.

In a book with so much discussion of giving, we explore a lot of truths that have to do with how we behave and the importance of obedience to God. But there are many gifts of sheer grace, many rewards that come just because God wants to bless us.

Yes, we want to fulfill the Great Commission. We want to go all over the world to serve him. But there are also aspects of all this that are, simply stated, wonderful moments of a loving Father saying, *Look what I have for you. I want to show you great things that so few others have seen. You are my child, and I love you.*

In those moments, he's not a *boss*. He's Abba, Father —a *daddy*.

Call on his name, and you'll understand.

TURNING ON THE POWER

All of the principles discussed in this book are wonderful and supernatural ... and they're not our work. They come through the power of God, dispensed by the Holy Spirit. Otherwise, we might as well be flashlights without batteries. Nothing could be more frustrating than finding a flashlight when the power goes off in your home—only to discover you have no working batteries.

That is an image of your life apart from the process of soaking, sowing, and flowing that comes through the Holy Spirit. It doesn't matter how much you want to be a "good Christian," or how many times you attend church, how much money you contribute, or how many good deeds you do—you will be as empty a vessel as the battery-less flashlight apart from the living Word of God flowing through you and empowering you by the Holy Spirit.

God wants each of us to shine in a dark world. He has told us we're the light of the world (Matthew 5:14). What a tragedy when the light of the world has no batteries! With a power source, that flashlight can light the way through a dark tunnel; without that source, it's a useless piece of plastic. And let's remember who owns the flashlight, and who decides where to point it. Our heavenly Father, the same one who placed his Spirit within us, will shine us in the right directions.

If you're a follower of Jesus Christ, you need not do anything special to invite the Holy Spirit into your life—he is there, just as sure as your heart was pumping blood through your body long before you learned about it in school. As you experience his presence, you can learn to cooperate with him, through reading the Word of God and asking him to illuminate it

> *You will be as empty as the battery-less flashlight apart from the living Word of God flowing through you and empowering you by the Holy Spirit.*

for you; by asking him to give you the right words during important conversations; and by relying on him to show you how to serve God as you go about the day. In time, you'll be more and more aware of the Spirit and how he works in your life. When you stumble, you'll feel his very gentle whisper of admonishment; when you are worried, you'll feel his word of encouragement; and when you're mourning, you'll feel his comfort. The Holy Spirit is more than just a power source; he is a friend in every need.

KingdomNomics

REQUIRES A CHRIST-CENTERED MENTALITY.

7

KINGDOM ATTITUDES

K*ingdomNomics* is looking at all of our resources in light of eternity. As we begin to make intentional decisions about our time, talent, and treasure, our attitudes about life begin to change as well. When we reflect upon the Scriptures, it's not long before we recognize that we see the world in a way that contrasts sharply from those who do not have God's view.

This is incredibly important because attitudes determine thoughts; thoughts govern feelings; and feelings guide actions. Those actions, of course, reinforce our attitudes, so that what we have in *KingdomNomics* is the opportunity to break negative cycles of behavior and begin positive ones. People, of course, try to do this every day, but it's simply not possible through the limits of human effort. One of the greatest insights of the Scriptures is validated through our simple observation of this world: No matter how hard we try, we fall into the same ruts. We make the same mistakes. We can't break the cycle of human sin—unless we allow Christ to break it for us.

So we're talking about a new set of attitudes, but attitudes that don't originate in our best intentions. They must come from the Spirit of God, living within us as believers.

Each one of us who accepts Christ as Savior will find that the Holy Spirit is now within us, and is working each day to reinforce these kingdom attitudes. Let's examine some of the major ones.

SUBMISSION: YIELDING TO GOD

Therefore, I urge you, brothers and sisters, in view of God's mercy, to offer your bodies as a living sacrifice, holy and pleasing to God—this is your true and proper worship.
Romans 12:1

In the passage above, we're encouraged to present ourselves to God as a living sacrifice. A sacrifice is something costly that is offered fully and without reservation. In the time of Paul, who wrote these words, animals were presented for sacrifice to God. But God had come in the flesh, through Jesus, to present *himself* as a living sacrifice for people. And in response, we present ourselves to him.

No longer are we slaves to legalistic, obligatory sacrifices. We are free to be joyful givers for the sake of righteousness.

This means that no longer are we slaves to legalistic, obligatory sacrifices. We are free to be joyful givers for the sake of righteousness. We don't make empty gifts with our hands, but full and loving gifts with our hearts in an "I want to obey" attitude toward God (Romans 6:17). It's the end of empty religion and the beginning of loving relationship. We are like the sailor who sets sail on the waters to take full advantage of the wind, not trying to force his own direction; we follow the wonderful winds of God's Spirit.

HUNGER: CONSUMING GOD'S WORD

Do not conform to the pattern of this world, but be transformed by the renewing of your mind. Then you will be able to test and approve what God's will is—his good, pleasing and perfect will.

Romans 12:2

This verse immediately follows the passage we just discussed, and the principle follows as well. As we are submissive to God's will, we find ourselves hungering for the nourishment that only the Word of God can bring us. The Word renews the mind. You'll notice that we really have two options: conformity or transformation. In conformity, we become one more product of a hopeless world; in transformation, we become more and more like Christ every day—more and more the person he has designed us to be.

We hunger for the Word once we see the power of its truth and its amazing effect on the life we live. Again, it's an "I want to" thing in that the more we experience the power of the Scriptures, the more of them we want. We actually develop a yearning for the only truth that can make such a difference, and we find ourselves committing it to memory, using it throughout the day in times of need. It's like putting on a special pair of glasses that show us our world as God sees it.

It can only happen as we soak our hearts in God's Word. David, the king, said that God's Word was more valuable to him than thousands of pieces of silver and gold (Psalm 19:10); Job said that he treasured it more than food (Job 23:12); and Jeremiah said that it *was* his food, he consumed it and let it become his heart's delight (Jeremiah 15:16). And Jesus said that his words are spirit and life (John 6:63).

Never think of the Bible as a book, or as paper and ink, or as word and paragraph. It is the living, eternal Word of God, a thing with no equal. It is as essential to life as oxygen, as healing as medicine.

HEAVEN-DRIVEN: A FOREVER MINDSET

Since, then, you have been raised with Christ, set your hearts on things above, where Christ is, seated at the right hand of God. Set your minds on things above, not on earthly things.

Colossians 3:1–2

Most people live completely in the here and now. As a matter of fact, it's a challenge for them to even plan for anything in the future. The principles

Gratitude keeps anxiety at bay.

of *KingdomNomics* don't stop with the future things on earth—those who practice *KingdomNomics* are motivated by eternity itself. As Paul writes, the things we see are temporary; they pass away, no matter how strong and real they seem at the time. But unseen things never pass away. (See 2 Corinthians 4:18).

This kingdom attitude, then, is a mindset. We should have a predisposition toward eternal reality. What does that mean? It means that once we look through the lens of how God sees this world, we act accordingly. We do things that the rest of the world may not understand at present, but that we know make sense in heavenly terms.

An earthly attitude is likely to be, *I would like to be comfortable today*. An eternal attitude would be, *I would like to be useful to God today, regardless of comfort*. An earthly attitude might be, *this new acquaintance is unlikely to be someone who can further my personal ambitions*. An eternal attitude will be, *this new acquaintance is beloved by God. What can I do to be his or her servant?*

Others cannot see past the visible; we seek to see what is invisible.

LOVE AND COMPASSION: THE PEOPLE FACTOR

For Christ's love compels us, because we are convinced that one died for all, and therefore all died.

2 Corinthians 5:14

This attitude involves finding more room in our life for others.

As we study the life of Jesus, we can't help but see that people came first for him—all kinds of people: the rich and the poor, the sick and the healthy, the righteous and the wicked. He loved them first and foremost because God loved them.

We are measured not by the love that comes most easily to us, but by the love that is sacrificial. Who is it hardest for you to love? Have you prayed to see that person as God does?

In *KingdomNomics*, we expect to grow in love and compassion with every day that goes by. Jesus said that this was how the world would know we are his people. We become less angry, less provoked than we once did. We are more willing to give. How? Compassion. Loving service brings us joy.

GRATITUDE: A THANKSGIVING SPIRIT

> *Though the fig tree does not bud and there are no grapes on the vines, though the olive crop fails and the fields produce no food, though there are no sheep in the pen and no cattle in the stalls, yet I will rejoice in the Lord, I will be joyful in God my Savior.*
> Habakkuk 3:17–18

Habakkuk's thought is irrational in the eyes of the world. Why rejoice over barren crops? Why thank God after a bad day at the office?

In *KingdomNomics*, we cultivate an attitude of gratitude in *all* things. "Rejoice in the Lord always. I will say it again: Rejoice!" (Philippians 4:4). Paul speaks of—and personally demonstrates—an attitude that has nothing to do with circumstances and everything to do with eternal reality. We rejoice because we're grateful for the goodness of God. The eternity-driven believer understands that life at its worst is filled with the blessings of God.

The Bible offers us a great abundance of reasons for rejoicing, and the more we soak our minds in them, the more we are changed. For example, gratitude keeps anxiety at bay (Philippians 4:6). Thanksgiving helps us put away foolish talk and coarse joking (Ephesians 5:4). Above all, rejoicing helps us see reality in eternal terms—filled with the goodness of God (1 Timothy 4:4). God responds to a grateful heart, and our gratitude overflows to God's glory (2 Corinthians 4:15).

People allow their resources to become burdens, when all that we have should be seen as blessings. When our spirits are transformed, and we begin to see life and the world through God's eyes, we feel truly free, truly joyful. We can't help but rejoice over our great God, over what he has done for

We aren't the owners, only the stewards, of our lives and possessions.

us, over what he allows us to do for him. We develop a kingdom attitude of gratitude, and it captures the attention and curiosity of others.

CONTENTMENT: GENUINE SATISFACTION

I know what it is to be in need, and I know what it is to have plenty. I have learned the secret of being content in any and every situation, whether well fed or hungry, whether living in plenty or in want.

Philippians 4:12

This kingdom attitude comes from the profound realization that God owns everything. If I own nothing, and he owns everything, why should I lose any sleep over the realm of "mine"? As Job observed, we are reduced to dust and ashes (Job 30:19). Physical things ultimately matter little in comparison to spiritual ones.

Thus, with that realization, Paul learned to be content in all things, whether in times of plenty or of want. He could sit under Roman house arrest and be filled with joy and gratitude, and therefore with utter contentment. For him, to live was Christ—in all things, in every moment—and to die was gain. To live meant that Christ came to be with him; to die meant that he would go to be with Christ. From the realization of that came a deep sense of well-being that the Roman rulers could not take away; that declining health could not take away; that *nothing* could touch.

> *The life of KingdomNomics is a life of daily faith that something wonderful is just around the corner.*

Contentment, then, is an overcoming kingdom attitude. It's total victory over the prison of circumstances. We aren't the owners, only the stewards, of our lives and possessions. We have nothing to lose but our chains, and that feels very good indeed. Our bodies themselves are not our own, and we can be content knowing that everything is on loan from God; the real joys come from eternal realities.

The contented believer even has a resilient spirit through the ups and downs of the state of the world. He knows that in all things God works for the good of those who know him and are called according to his purposes (Romans 8:28), and therefore current events cannot snatch away his joy either. Nothing that can happen is a surprise to God. No governments, no catastrophes, no dark trends are outside his power.

EXPECTANCY: FUTURE FAITH

*"Have faith in God," Jesus answered.
"Truly I tell you, if anyone says to this
mountain, 'Go, throw yourself into the
sea,' and does not doubt in their heart but
believes that what they say will happen, it
will be done for them."*

Mark 11:22–23

This verse describes the attitude of faithful expectancy that God is at work, and that, at every moment, he is about to do something new. We know that God never sleeps; he is always working, always moving people and events toward the culmination of his great purposes. Yet most people today don't believe in the miraculous. They might say they accept that God acts in the course of natural events, but if they ever recognized it happening, they would be totally taken by surprise. Most Christians don't live with a sense of godly anticipation.

And what happens? Faithlessness is a self-fulfilling prophecy. The New Testament tells us that Jesus saw the lack of faith in his hometown, and "he did not do many miracles there because of their lack of faith" (Matthew 13:58). We don't have because we don't ask; we don't expect.

So much of the joy of our life is in finding ourselves caught up in the great story that God is writing. Our daily time with him fills our spirits with a readiness to see him in action. It helps us see issues of eternal significance playing out in natural circumstances. And we're led to pray even more, asking God to let us be a part of what he is doing.

There are many more attitudes, all outlined in the Scriptures, but we'll stop here for the sake of brevity. The life of *KingdomNomics* is a life of daily faith that something wonderful is just around the corner. With God, this is always true. He "is able to do immeasurably more than all we ask or imagine, according to his power that is at work within us" (Ephesians 3:20).

KINGDOMNOMICS

REQUIRES AN INVESTMENT
IN GOD'S PLAN.

8

THE INVESTMENT PLAN

We have to have a plan! I might not phrase it quite as bluntly as the boxer Mike Tyson did, when he said, "Everybody has a plan until they get punched in the face," but he hits it right on the nose, doesn't he?

Most people travel through their younger years with superficial ideas about what they hope to accomplish. Mine were based on accumulation, on a more-cows-more-milk model that my father gave me. I seldom stopped to think about the *purpose* of having as much money and as many possessions as possible. How much would be enough? What would I do with all the money when I obtained it?

All roads eventually lead to specific destinations. I thought accumulation was my goal, but it was really only a road leading to ultimate destruction.

Once something bad happens, once we "get punched in the face," what then? Many people begin to operate in panic mode. The inept boxer will begin flailing wildly; the inept investor makes poor decisions.

When the great economic collapse of 2008 came, we saw that some had plans deep and strong enough to weather even the worst calamity; others panicked. For those with

77

goals no deeper than sheer accumulation, it was a time for despair. For others, who trusted God, it was merely a time to double down on prayer and seek his wisdom for the next step. If the stock market was their god, then it made sense for them to go to pieces. If they truly believed in Almighty God, however, then they knew that he still held the whole world in his hands.

Plan and purpose are concepts that flow beautifully through the entire Bible, from the moment God created the earth until the moment he brings history to a close in the final pages. There is nothing random or spontaneous about our God and his works. He is purposeful in all things: "But the plans of the LORD stand firm forever, the purposes of his heart through all generations" (Psalm 33:11).

> *If God has special things for me to do, then it follows that he must have given me special gifts or abilities to help me do them.*

Once we decide to place God at the center of our lives, then we realize that his purposes prevail, and it makes sense to adopt His plans for us. So a crucial *KingdomNomics* principle is to become a *purpose-driven* individual, to use the terminology of Rick Warren.

"Many are the plans in a person's heart, but it is the LORD's purpose that prevails" (Proverbs 19:21). This verse becomes a guiding principle for us. We realize that we'll have various plans and initiatives and objectives in life, but the key is to bring all of them into conformance with the Lord's great over-arching purpose. Some of our lesser plans won't fit, and they must be thrown out. Others he will bless, and he will nurture those toward bringing fruit.

It's intriguing to think of the great people of the Bible, and to see how their lives were dictated by clear plans God had for them:

The Jesus Plan:	To seek and to save the lost. (Luke 19:10)
The Paul Plan:	To preach the gospel to the Gentiles. (Acts 9:15)
The Abraham Plan:	To found a great nation to bless the earth. (Genesis 12:1-2)
The Moses Plan:	To bring the Israelites to the Land of Promise. (Exodus 3:8-10)

Even from a purely common sense point of view, we could agree that *history is written by men and women of strong and focused purpose*. From the Bible's point of view, it's crystal clear: God's kingdom is increased by men and women who tap into the purpose that God has for them. They understand that their story is part of a much bigger story, *his* story, and this great insight becomes their guiding light.

Here is how Paul expresses it: "For we are God's handiwork, created in Christ Jesus to do good works, which God prepared in advance for us to do" (Ephesians 2:10).

If God has special things for me to do, then it follows that he must have given me special gifts or abilities to help me do them. God is intentional in all that he does—he *always* has a plan, including the details of how I should be serving him. That means I have gifts and talents, and these are the leading indicators of what God wants me to do. Since I was reasonably good at the task of investing and building capital, I decided that

God wanted me to keep doing the same thing, but *with a mission*—with a focused purpose of what would be done with the accumulation.

No longer did I see money as a means of keeping score, or even of caring for my loved ones. Now it had a higher calling, as I myself did: it was about kingdom investment.

KNOWING THE PLAN

Perhaps the greatest verse in the Bible on the subject of God's will is this one: "For I know the plans I have for you," declares the LORD, "plans to prosper you and not to harm you, plans to give you hope and a future" (Jeremiah 29:11).

Consider what that one verse means for your life:

1. God has a plan perfectly formulated with your name on it.
2. It's a *good* plan. He didn't create you to be miserable, but to be fruitful.
3. God has reserved for you a future filled with hope.

Further, we can venture certain conclusions from this plan:

1. God's plan was written long before you were born. (Jeremiah 1:5)
2. God's plan for you is bound up with his plans for others. (Romans 8:28)
3. God's plan is built upon your gifts and talents. (Ephesians 2:10)
4. God's eternal purpose brings together your plan with those of others. (Proverbs 16:9)

5. God will guide you as you attempt to follow his plan. (Proverbs 16:3)

The Bible tells us, "Commit to the LORD whatever you do, and he will establish your plans" (Proverbs 16:3). All of this gives me great hope. If I soak in his presence, sow his Word to the Spirit, and let the Spirit flow through my mind and heart, I cannot fail

> *God always has a plan, including the details of how I should be serving him.*

to please him. He's not interested in hiding his will from me—why wouldn't he want me to know what he has in store for me?

So I'm freed to do what I do well, and to find out how I can please him with those skills. If I enjoy certain talents, it's because he made me to enjoy them so that I could serve him.

Then, as I make my plans in prayer and through the knowledge of the Word, he will guide me toward the things he wants me to do.

This makes my path straighter. It gives me clear goals and strong marching orders. It's very clear from reading the Bible what God wants: He wants, above all, to be reconciled to his children. We call this the Great Commission (Matthew 28:18-20). God's will is for us to go out to every part of the earth and make disciples. This includes next door and across the ocean.

Therefore, the first principle of my purpose is this: Somehow my personal plan will be linked into the Great Commission. It may not happen in a direct way, involving traditional missionary giving, for example (though I'll take part in that, too), but somehow or other, my investments are related to telling people about Jesus and sharing the plan of salvation with them.

Of course, as I've spent time with the Lord over the years, he has made *his* great desire *my* great desire. My greatest joy now is in telling people about Jesus. I invest in ministries and strategies that get Bibles into people's hands in the cities; the Word translated into languages where it's never been read or heard; the story of the gospel shown in the form of the "JESUS" film; all with the intention, along with the latest technologies and avenues that are now available, of communicating the good news of Jesus Christ.

I might also invest in plans to bring fresh water to villages that need it, where there are outbreaks of disease. I could be helping with a healthcare initiative, done in the name of Christ. These are things Jesus would have done when he was on earth and as he told the suffering people the good news of his plan for them. I might invest in schools and orphanages, because the Scriptures command us to care for orphans in their affliction.

> *"Gain all you can.*
> *Save all you can.*
> *Give all you can."*
> *John Wesley*

There are infinite ways of pleasing God and working toward his purpose. Much of my task as an investor, of course, is to use the same talents I used before I was investing with a mission: I look at "stock offerings," which are, in this case, Great Commission opportunities. I decide which ones will bear the most abundant fruit, which ones will bear perhaps some fruit, and which ones will bear no fruit (to use the terms Jesus uses in John 15).

Last Christmas, I spent some time thinking about the Magi, those visitors from the East who came to see the baby Jesus. They are more than simply colorful characters in our decorative manger scenes. History tells us that these men read the signs of the times, as God made available. They invested many months, and thousands of hard travel miles, to behold their young king. When that meeting occurred, they bowed in worship and offered their gifts worthy of a king. What they offered was a kingdom investment.

The Magi set an example for us. We know almost nothing about them other than their hearts of worship and their gifts. Perhaps it was the gifts of those visitors that financed the little family's trip to Egypt, where Jesus was safe from Herod's persecution. We can't know for sure.

But we can be certain God had a use for those gifts. For me, MAGI means *Money Advancing God's Investment*. I want to lay all that I have before the King.

KINGDOM INVESTMENT

John Wesley, founder of the Methodist Church, had a favorite sermon he loved to preach over the years. Its basic message was:

> Gain all you can.
> Save all you can.
> Give all you can.

Wesley began a frugal life style as a young man. As he grew older, his income began to increase quickly as his fame grew, but he maintained humble standards of living so that he could give more away. Even so, he realized that many of his followers, who were more devoted to business than he could be, would have opportunities to make much more money. He wanted them to realize that, as long as they did it honestly, Jesus would approve their business acumen. It would be useful to the kingdom.

When Wesley offered his three-point plan, he happened to be preaching about The Parable of the Shrewd Manager. In the story, Jesus said, "I tell you, use worldly wealth to gain friends for yourselves, so that when it is gone, you will be welcomed into eternal dwellings" (Luke 16:9).

Many people are surprised to read these words from Jesus. They think that somehow smart, shrewd business never intersects with kingdom behavior. Or they recall that famous occasion when Jesus walked through the temple with a whip, going after the money-lenders. In that situation, there were dishonest vendors at the temple, taking advantage of the poor (recorded in Matthew 21, Mark 11, and Luke 19). Jesus wasn't attacking commerce—he was attacking dishonesty, especially in a place of worship.

Jesus actually tells us, in Luke 16, to build a great network: "Gain friends." At the end of the day, of course, the kingdom of God is all about people. It's important to remember that all people are God's children and he loves them. Use business, he is saying, to build human relationships in which people can come to know him. Good business is kingdom business.

Therefore I try to stay as close to the Lord as I can, immersing myself in his Word and the flow of the Holy Spirit every day. I focus on his purposes, and ask him what he wants me to do, where he wants me to focus. In the course of the day, I continue to pray about opportunities to serve him in some way.

Meanwhile, I continue to be a good businessman, just as I always was. I try to gain all I can and save all I can, so that I can give all I can. I know in doing so that I'm walking the straight path that he set out for me. It's amazing just how many questions and puzzles and problems drain away from everyday existence when we know exactly what we're setting out to accomplish. I want

Ask God to help you create the clear, focused investment plan that serves him best.

consistently to do whatever honors God and pleases him. I want to invest my time and my resources with a Great Commission focus.

In a future chapter, we're going to talk about eternal investment—living and investing toward heaven, and that day when we'll see Christ face to face. But that's not the same as holding on to our resources until Jesus comes to call us home! No, when it comes to ministry and invest-ment and service, we must live very much in the *now*. In my family, we feel very strongly about giving while we are living. This is the *KingdomNomics* principle of *immediacy*.

I realize some people believe in letting their hold-ings do a great deal of work after they're gone—leaving endowments to colleges or churches or charities. These, of course, are generous uses of money, but when I focus on the Great Commission, on the people perishing every day without knowing Jesus, on people starving and with no clothes on their back, I can't see the wisdom of simply relying upon future trusts.

There's a great advantage in putting many of my resources to work right now, one of them being that I can guide the way they're used, without depending upon an executor to do so. And very selfishly, I can enjoy the pleasure of seeing the fruits of my investment and ministry of giving.

A great *KingdomNomics* principle, then, is to ask God to help you create the clear, focused investment plan that serves him best. You can be certain that He has your plan in mind.

Like a father who puts a brand new baseball glove high in the closet, awaiting that day some years from now when his infant son will grow into it, God has fashioned a wonderful course for you. He takes that same kind of joy that the father does as he says, "Let me show you how to throw a baseball." God couldn't wait to tell Abraham about his plan of blessing the whole world. He couldn't wait to let Paul know that he would be the one to take the gospel far beyond Jerusalem. And he has the same eagerness to tell you the special plan he has set out for you.

God has drawn up the plan. He has given you the gifts. And best of all, he will go along with you and help you fulfill it. Life is beautiful when it is focused, and when it is focused upon pleasing him. Believe me, it will please you, too.

KingdomNomics

IS BEING HEAVENLY MINDED AND EARTHLY SENSITIVE.

9

A RICHER EXPERIENCE

At the end of the last chapter, we touched on a certain paradox, even a tension that accompanies the life of any follower of Jesus Christ. It is the relationship between living for now and living for eternity.

We are made of flesh and blood, placed in bodies that will last a few decades before returning to dust. But we are unique among all living creatures in that we are spiritual beings as well. We have souls; we are made for eternity; and we survive the death of the body. Paul writes that "our citizenship is in heaven" (Philippians 3:20).

We hear a lot of talk about citizens and aliens these days. The truth is that we ourselves are citizens of another world, and even ambassadors of that world while we are here (2 Corinthians 5:20). This world is not the "main event" for us. Our true destination is an eternal one. Therefore we're never totally "at home" in this world; all human beings have an intuitive sense that there is another world, one that is greater—our heavenly home.

On the other hand, we don't sit waiting for heaven to begin. God has work for us to do here and now. We are here to bring glory to his name and people into his kingdom. The needs that we see in those people are spiritual needs, but there are physical ones, too. Jesus preached salvation, but he also healed the sick. He comforted the suffering and brought hope to people in despair. He brought heaven and earth, spirit and body, together in perfect harmony.

A fantastic *KingdomNomics* principle, then is to be heavenly minded and earthly sensitive. This precept guides my investment mission. I set my mind on eternal things, as the Scripture instructs me, but I live and work in the world around me based on perspectives from that heavenly world.

The effect is that it gives me a richer experience in my present life, because the light of heaven brightens my physical world, and I can bring the needs of my physical world before God on his throne in heaven. Kingdom living makes me feel truly alive, in spirit and in body.

It's a win/win situation—what Paul meant as he wrote his letter to the Philippians. He was under house arrest by the Romans at the time; aging and facing increasing health problems. He was

We have souls; we are made for eternity.

eager to be traveling and preaching, yet he couldn't leave the premises. And how did he respond? With a letter of incredible joy that pulsates from every page of Philippians. For one thing, he was experiencing God's presence. No chains could limit that. For another, he was ministering to people through letters, and even to the Roman guards. He knew that if he was in prison, then it was somehow part of God's purpose for him, so he never lost his hope. And here's what he said: "For to me, to live is Christ and to die is gain" (Philippians 1:21).

Win/win. To live, for him, was to experience Christ; to die was to go and *be with* Christ. Paul was a citizen of heaven, and therefore joyful on earth regardless of his circumstances.

If men can be joyful in Christ amidst the worst of circumstances, we can conclude that truly the experience of living this life should be rich and meaningful.

NEW KINDS OF JOY

I was hesitant about the name of this chapter. A *richer* experience? People would know that I'm an investor, and I worried they might think I was referring to earthly riches. There's certainly no shortage of poor teaching out there concerning the so-called "prosperity gospel." This is the twisting of the Word of God to make it appear that God cares more than anything else about making us wealthy and comfortable—as if the whole point of our faith were a selfish one.

You won't find that kind of teaching in this book about giving! When we speak of a richer experience, we have a broader meaning of rich in spirit. We're discussing new kinds of joy that would never be possible apart from investing our lives in the kingdom of God. We don't set out to please ourselves—we set out to please God. But in the end, we find happiness, contentment, purpose, and fulfillment. And it seems to happen precisely because we are living in ways that non-believers would never experience.

Cheerful giving simply doesn't happen in a greed-driven life—and I speak as someone who has struggled with greed in the past. I still have to be on my guard to keep it from raising its ugly head in my life. When we live for worldly values, the petty things we pursue produce petty rewards. But when we live with a kingdom perspective, the rewards are gracious and surprising.

For example, one year I received my tax refund shortly after the beginning of the year. I looked at the refund amount and thought, *No, that can't be right*. But I checked my records and found out that sure enough, the government was refunding me, almost to the penny, the sum I had given to God's work the entire year! I had to laugh. It was one of those moments when God seemed to "show his hand" so to speak. I didn't give with any thought of getting it back somehow; I gave from my heart. But God was saying, *Now, let me bless you a little bit!*

> *When we live for worldly values, the petty things we pursue produce petty rewards. But when we live with a kingdom perspective, the rewards are gracious and surprising.*

That's unlikely to happen more than once. Next time it will be something else entirely. But that's part of the pleasure—finding new kinds of joy that come simply from being obedient to God. As you grow in maturity, you will no longer think of giving as being some kind of sacrificial obligation that is "painful." It would be more painful by far *not* to give, because you'd be robbing yourself of the pleasure of thinking about what God was going to do with your gift.

The key is that you come to view a giving transaction as an investment rather than a "loss." Nothing done in God's name ever passes away; it leaves a mark in eternity. If you give to help Christian literature be distributed in China, for example, you think, *Someone may come to Christ because of this check I'm writing. I may meet that person in the next life! God may actually be enlarging the population of heaven with this gift.*

That's a powerful thought, and it only makes you want to be more generous. It's no wonder that God loves a cheerful giver. He sees the joy each giver is experiencing, and he shares it. And he uses the gift for his purposes.

NEW FREEDOM

There are not only new kinds of joy, but new kinds of freedom. I've noticed that one of the most powerful effects of giving is that it actually causes greed to subside. Let's agree that greed is a substantial problem in today's world. One of the worst parts is that we don't even realize it. A PBS TV special coined the term "Affluenza"—the disease of having so much that we don't see its power over us.

This world is not the "main event" for us.

Pastor Tim Keller tells how he had planned to preach a series on the Seven Deadly Sins. As he listed them for his wife and came to greed, his wife said, "You'll have the smallest attendance on the day you preach that one."

When he asked her why, she replied, "Most of us don't think it's our problem."

And she was right. No one was excited about a greed sermon. Keller realized that, in all his years of counseling, no one had ever come to him and asked him to help them with the problem of greed.

We don't think of it as sin; we think of it as *normal.* Greed can be very powerful without our realization. There have been times in my life when I heard that quiet whisper, *More, more, more.* Nothing will more quickly take our eyes off God. Even when I begin with the principle of kingdom investment, I can get caught up in the dollar figures, the money game, the acquisition of sums, and I realize I'm being motivated by greed rather than good.

But then I give the money to God. I feel what I call the "I want to give" attitude come surging back. Then he comes to me and says, *Here, let me show you how I'm going to use it—you'll love this!* And I always do. The joy of obedience causes the sin of greed to lose its grip.

> **KingdomNomics**
> *relates to my desire not to forfeit the grace that could be mine, simply out of some unworthy human desire to hang onto some item in this world that could become an idol.*

As we give, we are also freed from the prison of self. Earlier in this book we discussed the self-service world we live in. Just as greed seems like the default attitude for ordinary people, self-absorption is taken completely for granted. Remember those magazine articles we discussed in Chapter Five? None of them offer to tell you "Ten Ways to Serve Your Neighbor" or "How to Nurture an Attitude of Humility."

Giving does something remarkable. It makes you self-forgetful. For one thing, you meet new and wonderful people. Some of them are fellow sponsors of good work; others are people you may be helping. There are new friends, and there are hurting people with issues that keep your own feelings of self-pity in check. Greed knocks life out of perspective, while giving shows you the world through Christ's eyes. One reason people feel so uniquely alive on overseas mission trips, or on local service projects, is that they're freed from the prison of self-obsession. Their eyes are wider, their ears are more open, their senses are more attuned to what God is doing in the world.

It's possible, of course, to become self-righteous in giving. Jesus warned about the hypocrites of his time who did their good deeds in public, so that they might be seen. But genuine, generous giving—so often quiet and anonymous—helps us to experience God and know his joy.

Once again, you can look at your checkbook for a definitive biography. If its register reveals that all your investments are for personal pleasure, you're one kind of person; if more of the entries have to do with generosity, it's very unlikely that you are a self-absorbed individual. My experience in life suggests to me that one of the most difficult quests in all of life is the quest to be humble or unselfish. The problem is you can be proud of your humility, and an unselfish act can focus you on self!

The very best remedy for greed is kingdom giving. You're freed from that particular dungeon, and the outside air smells sweet indeed.

CONSUMED: THE ONLY WAY TO GO

In short, *KingdomNomics* relates to my desire not to forfeit the grace that could be mine, simply out of some unworthy human desire to hang onto some item in this world that could become an idol. If it all belongs to him, then how does my clutching at things affect my spirit?

So I return frequently to the King's table, and I keep my heart hungry for him. Sometimes the visits must be brief—just a snack from his Word—but I will always be back, because the fact is that I am *consumed* by this relationship with Christ.

I don't want to be like the people from that lukewarm church profiled in Revelation 3:15-16. God told those people that their works were neither hot nor cold, but lukewarm, so that he wanted to vomit them from his mouth. I want my words and thoughts and deeds to be aflame!

Therefore my role models are those figures in the Scriptures who were absolutely consumed with the desire to know God better. I will mention only a few of them.

- **Abram:** "After this, the word of the LORD came to Abram in a vision: 'Do not be afraid, Abram. I am your shield, your very great reward'" (Genesis 15:1). Abram learned from God that this relationship was the most important factor in his life. He learned that God is the God who provides, and that a relationship with him rates a priority far beyond any other blessing that a person can possibly have in this world.

- **Job:** "Yes, the Almighty will be your gold And your precious silver; For then you will have your delight in the Almighty, And lift up your face to God" (Job 22:25–26, NKJV). Also, "I have not departed from the commandment of His lips; I have treasured the words of His mouth More than my necessary food" (Job 23:12, NKJV). Job teaches us that everything is sourced in God. Knowing him is greater than any earthly treasure. God himself is our wealth. When misfortune began to consume Job, it had no ultimate effect, because Job was consumed by God.

- **David:** "For with You is the fountain of life; in your light we see light" (Psalm 36:9). David was a mighty king. He had wealth of every kind at his disposal. And yet for him, all of life, all of light came from God and God alone. He wrote, "Whom have I in heaven but You? And there is none upon earth that I desire besides You" (Psalm 73:25, NKJV). David had his eyes on the eternal realities of life—only God ultimately makes a difference for us.

- **Solomon:** "For those who find me find life, and receive favor from the LORD" (Proverbs 8:35). Solomon was referring to the words of wisdom from the mouth of God. One who listens to the words of wisdom from God not only finds life, but also obtains favor from God. Solomon, too, had great wisdom and wealth and power, yet he knew that there was one source of life and meaning and goodness.

- **Jesus Christ:** "It is the Spirit who gives life; the flesh profits nothing. The words that I speak to you are spirit, and they are life" (John 6:63, NKJV). Who but the Son of God himself can provide a better model for us? Jesus tells us that the Spirit gives life. Jesus said, "My food is to do the will of him who sent me, and to finish his work" (John 4:34). Jesus was consumed by the desire to please and serve his heavenly Father.

- **Paul:** "Not that I have already obtained all this, or have already been made perfect, but I press on to take hold of that for which Christ Jesus took hold of me. Brothers, I do not consider myself yet to have taken hold of it. But one thing I do: Forgetting what is behind and straining toward what is ahead, I press on toward the goal to win the prize for which God has called me heavenward in Christ Jesus" (Philippians 3:12–14, NIV84). Paul nicely summarizes the "consumed" life—pushing heavenward with every moment and every impulse, fully devoted to pleasing God.

KingdomNomics

IS KINGDOM DRIVEN.

10

THE PATH TO SIGNIFICANCE

A fair question that many people may ask is this: "What does my life have to do with that of a little girl in China? A young doctor in Kenya? An old grandmother in Brazil?"

For me, the answer is: "I just can't help myself."

Let me explain why.

When we begin to follow Christ, and begin to soak our minds and hearts in his Word, we begin a process of total change, becoming like Christ. The Holy Spirit begins a long makeover process that lasts the rest of our lives. We "are being transformed into his image with ever-increasing glory, which comes from the Lord, who is the Spirit" (2 Corinthians 3:18). We no longer conform to this world and its ideas. Instead, we seek to be transformed by the renewing of our minds (Romans 12:2).

We're told this many times in the New Testament. As we cooperate with the work of the Spirit, we begin to resemble Jesus more and more each day, seeing our surroundings as he sees them; responding as he would respond. We help the process along by daily decisions to "put on" Christ—as we might don our daily attire. "Clothe yourselves with the Lord Jesus Christ, and do not think about how to gratify the desires of the flesh" (Romans 13:14).

There have been many occasions when I've realized I was thinking an unworthy thought, or developing an attitude that would not please my Lord. When I catch myself doing that, I make a decision of the will to let Christ take charge. It's like getting out of my chair, walking across the room, and putting on a white jacket that completely changes my appearance—except that "putting on Christ" changes me on the inside. I can choose to have his mindset, through the Holy Spirit. I take on his attitudes, and the unworthy ones melt away.

Over time, as this happens, our values begin to resemble his. One of those values is caring for the world. We can't be small-minded anymore, caring only about ourselves, our family, our cozy neighborhood. God loves the world, and so do we. He gave his only son, and we give our only lives. We feel connected to our brothers and sisters in Christ all across the globe, and we want everyone else to have a chance to respond to the gospel.

> *As we cooperate with the work of the Spirit, we begin to resemble Jesus more and more each day.*

In addition to that, we know that Jesus has given us his marching orders, known as the Great Commission. He wants us to go to every corner of this planet and share the good news with every single individual. It's one of the last things he told his disciples before leaving this world, and we can assume he saved his most important words for last.

So yes, we care about the other side of town, and we care about the other side of the world. As a matter of fact, if you can handle this idea, we even care about people in those nations who despise our faith and despise our country—those with whom our country may be at war. Jesus told us to pray for our enemies. He forgave the very men who nailed him to a cross, and died for them.

These attitudes can seem strange to non-believers, perhaps, but they're the attitudes Jesus modeled so that his followers would adopt them. I can tell you that, after years of serving him, I'm still working every day to live them out.

So yes, I care about people across the world. I can't help myself!

Every now and then, someone realizes that followers of Jesus have unique hearts. In 2011, the *New York Times* ran an editorial by a writer who had a good word for evangelical Christians. He admitted that followers of Jesus are often stuck with stereotypes of being small-minded and hypocritical; and he said that sometimes those labels may be well-earned. On the other hand, he wrote:

> Evangelicals are disproportionately likely to donate 10 percent of their incomes to charities, mostly church-related. More important, go to the front lines, at home or abroad, in the battles against hunger, malaria, prison rape, obstetric fistula, human trafficking or genocide, and some of the bravest people you meet are evangelical Christians (or conservative Catholics, similar in many ways) who truly live their faith.
>
> I'm not particularly religious myself, but I stand in awe of those I've seen risking their lives in this way—and it sickens me to see that faith mocked at New York cocktail parties.[5]

Small-minded people have not taken on the mind of Christ. Those who have the mind of Christ have developed the kingdom attitude of caring about significance and impact.

DEEP GLADNESS

Author and theologian Frederick Buechner has said that God calls you to that place where your deep gladness meets the world's deep need. This is, again, how we're wired. In the beginning, we discover that we have a God-shaped hole in our hearts—nothing fills it but him. Then, as we accept his lordship, we find a new empty place. This one is in the shape of the people he loves. It will be filled and galvanized by the mission he has given us.

So we don't pursue impact for the ordinary reasons of fame or impressing someone. We don't pursue it out of sense of obligation. We're chasing that deep gladness that comes when we address the needs God has set before us.

Everywhere on earth, from mansions to slums, from deserts to cities, there are people suffering. They may be hungry; they may be sick; they simply may not have heard the saving truth about Jesus. These people are God's children. If you're a parent, think of how you feel about your kids. When they're in pain, you're in pain. You would do anything, pay any price, to alleviate their suffering. You would even take their pain upon yourself if you could.

That's what God has done for us in Christ. He provided a way out of our suffering. And it is what he does through you and through me, to make that way available to all of his children.

So impact is important to us. The believer who stays in his prayer closet communing with God, or who lives as a "rabbit hole Christian"—hopping from Bible study to Bible study to church committee meeting, his path never intersecting with needy people or with mission of any kind—is missing something. He was created to have an impact in this world.

God has a process for preparing us for impact. It's best told in the Parable of the Talents (to use the term of the NIV84) in Matthew 25. A *talent*, in the language of those times, was a unit of weight for measuring money—like saying "a pound of gold," for example. In the parable, three servants were given money based on their abilities, and rewarded based on their investments. The master says to the most effective of the investors, "Well done, good and faithful servant! You have been

> *"Putting on Christ" changes me on the inside. I can choose to have his mindset.*

faithful with a few things; I will put you in charge of many things. Come and share your master's happiness!" (Matthew 25:21).

Deep gladness is the sharing of the Master's happiness that comes from using our resources for the things God intended. One of the servants was given just a little bit, and he played it safe; he buried his talents in the ground. This is not God's desire. He wants us to take what we have and multiply it. If you have people-related talents—network. If you have financial resources—invest. If you have creative talents—expand them so that, in some way, the most possible people have an opportunity to become followers of Jesus.

That's what my family's mission is all about. We want to take whatever we have, increase it exponentially as far as it will go, and have as wide a godly impact on this world as we possibly can. That's our life, our deepest gladness; it's what we live for.

As I have opportunity to talk to younger believers, I counsel them to be faithful in the small things. It begins with teaching our children to put a quarter in the collection plate, or to provide a little allowance money toward our family's project to help a child overseas through a mission agency. This plants the seeds of the joy of giving to God's kingdom, and allows our children to go from smaller things to medium things, and someday to greater things. It has been said that big oak trees grow from little acorns.

> *Deep gladness is the sharing of the Master's happiness that comes from using our resources for the things God intended.*

We see this pattern in the lives of great Christian leaders through the centuries who have ultimately had an impact upon the world because of their obedience and their godly vision. As they have passed on, we know that God has welcomed them to heaven with the words, "Well done, good and faithful servant! Come and share your Master's happiness."

KINGDOM LOGISTICS

God's process also involves kingdom logistics. This happens as he moves the Word of God from the bookshelf to the mind, where it takes root; to the human heart, where it sprouts into solid conviction; and to the hands, where it takes effect in this world.

Logistics are about fine details: planning, implementation, and coordination. They literally make dreams come true. We want to win our world for Christ—but how? Where to begin? What kind of process? Who will help us? Where will the funding come from? How will we address obstacles?

Some of the most visionary leaders aren't detail-oriented people, and some of the most detail-oriented people need dreamers around them to give them purpose and direction. In kingdom logistics, God brings us all together to work for the common purpose of fulfilling the Great Commission. Your gift may seem small taken alone, but it fits into his plan; it only needs to snap into place beside the gifts of others.

The great plan, in all its fine detail, begins in the very heart of God. Just as he has always had a plan for each one of us, as we've seen, he also has always had a plan for how we will coordinate with each other. We tend to think of ourselves as individuals, and we are. But we are also part of the immense tapestry, the big picture of God carrying out his purpose through human history.

> *"Give up your small ambitions." This life is all you have. Why not live it for the greatest possible goal?*

God's heart takes the form of his Word. And, as he says, "My word that goes out from my mouth ... will not return to me empty, but will accomplish what I desire and achieve the purpose for which I sent it" (Isaiah 55:11). So we find our great sense of life purpose in locating our precise place in that tapestry, what our role must be, who else it must involve, and where it must be carried out.

His plan is perfect from his perspective. From ours, of course, it is full of bottlenecks, empty slots, seemingly unbreakable walls, and dire personnel shortages. Think of how it must have appeared to the first generation of Christians, when Christ had no followers outside of Jerusalem. He had told them to go to the whole world, and anyone would have called that goal insane. Two thousand years later, Christians make up as much as a third of the world. At those New York cocktail parties mentioned earlier, they'll tell you our faith is on the retreat, all but ready to be discarded as some relic of old times.

The truth is, the worldwide number of believers has nearly quadrupled in the last one hundred years, from six hundred million to two billion.[6] Yes, in this modern, technological world, God is more on the move than ever.

No matter how much people scoff,

God is working his purpose out
as year succeeds to year:
God is working his purpose out,
and the time is drawing near;
nearer and nearer draws the time,
the time that shall surely be,
when the earth shall be filled with the glory of God
as the waters cover the sea.
Arthur Campbell Ainger, traditional hymn

This is why kingdom investment always points toward world impact. When it comes to thinking of the big picture, we just can't help ourselves. When it comes to thinking of people finding the hope and salvation of Christ, our deep gladness is engaged. When it comes to making it all happen, we turn to kingdom logistics.

"For the eyes of the LORD range throughout the earth to strengthen those whose hearts are fully committed to him" (2 Chronicles 16:9). Our eyes and our thoughts should range through the earth as well, and we should be fully committed to him.

In that way, God's purposes move from his heart to our hands and feet to implementation across the globe. And once we see that happen, once we experience the incredible thrill of playing some part in it, we'll no longer be satisfied simply by lying on a beach, or settling for smaller pleasures.

As Frances Xavier once put it, "Give up your small ambitions." This life is all you have. Why not live it for the greatest possible goal?

KingdomNomics

HAS A FOREVER FOCUS.

11

ETERNAL DIVIDENDS

T he movie *Gladiator* opens with a scene in which the Roman General Maximus is getting his troops excited before they go into battle against barbarians in Germany. He rides his horse back and forth at the head of the line, and he shouts so that all his troops can hear him, "What we do in life echoes in eternity!"

This statement is true on every battlefield, whether in a deep forest with the Roman army or in the ordinary decisions you make in the course of each day. *What happens here has eternal repercussions.*

This is our final *KingdomNomics* principle: We live for eternal results, for ultimate glory.

Most people don't understand the Bible's view of eternity. They understand that there is a physical world, the one in which we live and age and finally die. And they realize there is the eternal world that follows, bound by heaven and hell, but not physical locations or the passing of time. They see it as a "someday" place, something not really real until we get there.

Yes, there really is a physical heaven, where God is and where we will see him face to face. Paul says that "for now we see only a reflection as in a mirror; then we shall see face to face. Now I know in part; then I shall know fully, even as I am fully known" (1 Corinthians 13:12). So we know that heaven will be wonderful, and there will be no more mysteries.

However, it's important to understand that eternal reality isn't confined to being a *someday* thing. It is also a *now* thing. Paul's letter to the Ephesians speaks of the "heavenly realms," refer-

We live for eternal results, for ultimate glory.

ring to these mysterious "realms" five times. He means the eternal reality, the true nature of things that our human eyes cannot see. Here are some key facts, as revealed in that letter:

- Our spiritual blessings are in the heavenly realms. (Ephesians 1:3)
- Christ rules there. (Ephesians 1:20)
- God has raised believers to sit beside Christ there. (Ephesians 2:6)
- The work of the church occurs there. (Ephesians 3:10)
- There are dark forces at work there, too— spiritual warfare. (Ephesians 6:12)

You may look at yourself in a mirror and think, "I'm not much to look at, and I have bad habits, and there are a million things wrong with me." But in the reality of the heavenly realms, you are perfect—because you are cleansed of every sin and forgiven. When God looks at you, he sees the perfection of Christ. The heavenly realms are the true spiritual reality of things.

While Ephesians gives us the most detailed information on this subject, virtually every page of the New Testament echoes the wisdom that what we do here is bound up in eternity. Eternity is real; eternity is now; and what we do here makes a difference there.

Yes, we've saved the most fascinating and perhaps difficult teachings about the kingdom for last. This world is not all there is; what we see before us is genuine and it's very important, but it's not the ultimate reality! It's not even the *lasting* reality. All that we see will pass away, but we happen to be eternal creatures; heaven is our true destiny. The heavenly realms reflect our spiritual condition.

So we live accordingly. "Since, then, you have been raised with Christ, set your hearts on things above, where Christ is, seated at the right hand of God. Set your minds on things above, not on earthly things. For you died, and your life is now hidden with Christ in God" (Colossians 3:1–3).

MOTIVES MATTER

There are so many implications to what that means for you and me that we would need many more books just to begin discussing them all. However, for now, let's focus on the fact that when we realize the truth of these things, we know we must choose where we invest ourselves. Every day is filled with choices. And it's not just about the decisions you make, but why you make them.

In the Sermon on the Mount, Jesus had plenty to say about actions and their motives. He spoke of doing good things for the wrong reasons. He said, "Be careful not to practice your righteousness in front of others to be seen by them. If you do, you will have no reward from your Father in heaven" (Matthew 6:1).

But why? Shouldn't we be rewarded for doing something good? The key is in the words *to be seen by them*. Remember, the heavenly world is the world of ultimate reality. Appearances don't matter there—it's all about the true spiritual nature of things.

Jesus goes on to talk about the hypocrites who give showy prayers in public, letting everyone know about their giving. His point is that these people have already received their reward in full. When we do things for the kingdom, which is invisible, our reward is in heaven.

This is why Paul tells us that God "has blessed us in the heavenly realms with every spiritual blessing in Christ" (Ephesians 1:3). The real blessings, the real rewards, are not of this world. They are eternal; they are invisible.

You might ask, "Well, why would I want to do anything for *invisible* rewards? Isn't that like being paid in imaginary money?"

I would turn the question back in your direction—why do anything for rewards that are fleeting?

Here's the way Jesus puts it:

> *Do not store up for yourselves treasures on earth, where moths and vermin destroy, and where thieves break in and steal. But store up for yourselves treasures in heaven, where moths and vermin do not destroy, and where thieves do not break in and steal. For where your treasure is, there your heart will be also.*
>
> Matthew 6:19–21

The things we do for God and his kingdom are ever-lasting. You've probably heard the phrase that "integrity is who you are when no one's looking." The fact is that there is never such a time. *God* is always looking. When you do some act of evil, and you think it has gone unnoticed, it has not. When you quietly commit an act of kindness, or make an anonymous donation, it's not anonymous to God.

Oscar Hammerstein, who wrote the words to many great Broadway musicals, wrote about a picture he saw that was taken by someone who flew over the Statue of Liberty in a helicopter. He marveled at the precision of the hairs that were sculpted on Lady Liberty's head. He realized that when the statue was sculpted by the French as a gift to America, there were no helicopters. The

> *Every day is filled with choices. And it's not just about the decision you made, but why you made it.*

sculptor could not have had any idea that the human eye would ever behold his fine, careful work at the top of the great statue. He would never have labored over individual hairs if he was working for the opinions of people. [7] It had to be an act of pure artistry.

God, of course, was in a position to see that artist's work. He is in a position to see everything that is done. He numbers the hairs on our own heads. Therefore we must stop living for the opinions of others, and begin living for the opinion of heaven, where the heart is known for what truly lies inside it.

As I go about my kingdom investing, I must stop and consider this principle constantly. Why am I giving? Could it be pride? Could it be for the applause of others? Has my giving simply become another money game?

All of these are possible if the "old" Phil sneaks up and slips into my heart. It helps to spend time with God each day, soaking my mind and heart in his Word. It also helps to come into contact with the needs that people have, the causes to which I'm giving. When I see people coming to Christ, or the hungry being fed, or a village getting a fresh-water well for the first time, my motives fall into line. I feel the "flowback of the Holy Spirit," and I find a powerful joy in serving God because I love him and I love his children.

THE KEY IS FAITH

We are surrounded by what we can see and hear and touch. How, then, do we begin to live for what we can't? Isn't that difficult?

Yes, it can be difficult when we're out of step with God's Spirit. But the key is to live by faith: "Now faith is confidence in what we hope for and assurance about what we do not see" (Hebrews 11:1). The key words here are *confidence* and *assurance*, or conviction. Our faith is based on truth, not some vague aspiration. We *know* God is good. We *know* Christ has defeated death and broken open the door to that eternal world, and we live based on that. We may serve an invisible world, but we see that world with our hearts.

> *The things we do for God and his kingdom are everlasting.*

The writer of Hebrews goes on to say that "without faith it is impossible to please God, because anyone who comes to him must believe that he exists and that he rewards those who earnestly seek him" (Hebrews 11:6). The writer lists the great heroes of the Old Testament who served God. But he ends the chapter with a remarkable statement.

> *These were all commended for their faith, yet none of them received what had been promised, since God had planned something better for us so that only together with us would they be made perfect.*
>
> Hebrews 11:39–40

In other words, these people weren't going after earthly rewards, and they didn't receive them. They understood that "God had planned something better for us." Elsewhere, the writer makes the same point, that there was no earthly reward for these people, yet it was all right with them, because they understood they were "foreigners and strangers on earth." They were longing for a better country—a heavenly one. "Therefore God is not ashamed to be called their God, for he has prepared a city for them" (Hebrews 11:13–17).

I'm highly motivated by the idea of being the kind of person of whom God is not ashamed to be called his master. Therefore I'm willing to look upon myself as just visiting this planet. My home is in heaven, and like the people described in that chapter in Hebrews, I'm longing for my home country. I'm longing for the city God has prepared for me, and it is that city that gets my best attention here, my best service.

I have a forever focus. Therefore I live by faith and not by sight. I align my life with rules and standards that don't always fit in with those of this world. I don't seek to have all my reward here, though there are, in fact, many rewards even in this life. God is good now, and he is good in the heavenly realms. The richest blessings are in Christ and in the spiritual reality, but as for here, I have no complaints either.

Paul sums it up for us:

> *So we fix our eyes not on what is seen, but on what is unseen, since what is seen is temporary, but what is unseen is eternal.*
>
> 2 Corinthians 4:18

KINGDOM INVESTMENT

I believe that kingdom investment results in sending money to heaven. In chapter eight we discussed The Parable of the Shrewd Manager. Jesus was making the point in the story that spiritually-minded people often don't realize they should be sharp and intelligent in the way they handle their money—just like non-spiritually-minded people. Effective management is no sin.

As a matter of fact, the manager in the story was actually dishonest—which Jesus was in no way recommending. The point was that the manager was quick-witted. Jesus said,

> *The master commended the dishonest manager because he had acted shrewdly. For the people of this world are more shrewd in dealing with their own kind than are the people of the light. I tell you, use worldly wealth to gain friends for yourselves, so that when it is gone, you will be welcomed into eternal dwellings.*
>
> Luke 16:8–9

This is one of several parables involving an unscrupulous character who still has a specific behavior that Jesus says we can learn from. Here he is making the point that the only real use of money is to make an impact on eternity.

When I first read this parable, it was exciting to me because it told me I could keep wearing my "investor cap" and use my best skills—but now, for God's kingdom. I didn't have to live by the philosophy that I once heard put this way: "Make as much as you can, save as much as you can—then sit on your can." That's a warped version of the Wesley quote we discussed earlier. For some reason, many Christians feel they should be allergic to wise investment, so they stash their money away like the fellow in the parable who buried his talents in the ground.

I want to give as much as I can, as frequently as I can, for the most God-pleasing purposes I can, in as many different settings as I can.

Not me! I want to give as much as I can, as frequently as I can, for the most God-pleasing purposes I can, in as many different settings as I can. I understand that what I bind on earth is bound in heaven, that any God-pleasing act is a victory in the invisible world: the heavenly realms. You may say, "How does it change anything if you support a hungry child in Kenya?" I will say that it causes the angels to stand up and cheer. Jesus says, "There is rejoicing in the presence of the angels of God over one sinner who repents" (Luke 15:10). We're also told that when we feed or clothe "the least of these," it's as if we have done that for Jesus (Matthew 25:40). That gives me a lot of opportunities to do something nice for Jesus, who has given his all for me.

When I read those references to angels rejoicing in heaven, my heart leaps within me. I long to be in such a place, where there are raucous celebrations over each good thing that happens on earth. I can't be there now—not in the body—but I'm there in spirit. And my investments can go there. That's why I'm sending ahead as many of them as I can. They say you can't take it with you, and that's certainly true. What they forget to mention, however, is that you can send it on ahead. That's what the shrewd manager does. One who has studied *KingdomNomics* will do the same. It's kingdom investment: what we do in life echoes in eternity.

KingdomNomics

IS USING WHAT IS TEMPORAL AND
LEVERAGING IT FOR ETERNITY.

12

DEVELOPING YOUR INVESTMENT PORTFOLIO

As I write the finishing paragraphs for this book, I'm listening to accounts of yet another "Storm of the Century." Extreme weather, as we've all noticed, has become a distressingly frequent theme in the news.

Yet we could also say that extreme *everything* is happening. We're still recovering from an extreme recession. We live in a nation that is extremely divided politically. We live with the knowledge that religious extremists in another part of the world are looking for ways to strike at us through terror. It's clear that we live in times of turbulence. Each following day on the calendar looms as a question mark. We surely can't build a foundation of hope based upon our market investments. I see people coming to grips with that fact even if they've never opened a Bible. It's simple common sense.

We don't place our hope in financial wealth, but we see it as a way to take action on an active daily basis.

But for those of us who believe the Scriptures, nothing has really changed. We have always known that this world is not forever, that our Lord will return "like a thief in the night," sometime when we least expect him.

As a result, we must live each day asking ourselves, "What if today were my last day? How would I want to spend it? What would my kingdom investment portfolio look like?"

We can't afford to take our eyes off the Lord and his Word. And we can't afford to delay in acting upon our convictions. This is one of the supreme reasons my family believes in "giving while we're living." I'm not trying to be morbid or alarmist. I simply take seriously the possibility that I could wake up some morning to a truly cataclysmic event: a mushroom cloud over some part of our nation, a terrorist attack powerful enough to shake our infrastructure to its foundation, or a total worldwide financial meltdown. I've labored to be a good steward and create wealth, and I want to send it to the kingdom in good time, lest it become worthless paper.

> *We should be just as deliberate and intentional about what we give as we are about what we earn.*

Then again, I do have considerations on "this side," too. I need to take care of my family. "Anyone who does not provide for their relatives, and especially for their own household, has denied the faith and is worse than an unbeliever" (1 Timothy 5:8). This means I must be thoughtful and balanced in my decision making, giving what I can and living as if today *may* be the last day, yet being ready to care for my family if there is indeed a tomorrow, as there has been every day up to this one. As long as there is any doubt, I must keep investing wisely and multiplying my investment, in line with the principles of Jesus for fruitfulness and multiplication.

I try to live sensibly and wisely as the proverb suggests: "Keep falsehood and lies far from me; give me neither poverty nor riches, but give me only my daily bread. Otherwise, I may have too much and disown you and say, 'Who is the LORD?' Or I may become poor and steal, and so dishonor the name of my God" (Proverbs 30:8–9). Talk about "extremes"—those are the two bookend mistakes to avoid. On the one side, we could attain enough wealth to become arrogant; on the other, enough poverty to become dishonest. Wise living, of course, allows us to honestly earn enough to get our daily bread and still give to purposes that honor God. Paul reflects that very kind of balance: "I have learned to be content whatever the circumstances. I know what it is to be in need, and I know what it is to have plenty. I have learned the secret of being content in any and every situation, whether well fed or hungry, whether living in plenty or in want. I can do all this through him who gives me strength" (Philippians 4:11–13).

This is the mindset we use to try to navigate the turbulent waters of these times. We don't place our hope in financial wealth, but we see it as a way to take action on an active daily basis.

THE GREAT RACE

What, then, is this earthly life, if the next one is our true destiny?

The Bible characterizes it as a great race toward a finish line that marks the beginning of the fullness of eternal life—heaven itself. In Hebrews we read, "Let us run with endurance the race that is set before us" (Hebrews 12:1, NKJV).

In order to run a race, we need to know where we're running and why. I like to think of this great race described in Hebrews in this way:

R — REVELATION: INSIGHT

A — ACCEPTANCE: ASSIMILATION OF THE VISION

C — CONVICTION: CROWN (run with conviction for a crown).

E — ENVISIONING: EYES FIXED ON ETERNAL VALUES

As I run my race, is there a way I can take what is temporal and leverage it for the advancement of the kingdom with resultant eternal value?

I believe the answer to this last question is a resounding yes.

We are racing through the temporal toward our eternal home. "For our citizenship is in heaven, from which we also eagerly wait for the Savior, the Lord Jesus Christ" (Philippians 3:20, NKJV). Hebrews 13:14 tells us that we are heading toward an eternal city; toward "an inheritance that can never perish, spoil or fade. This inheritance is kept in heaven for you" (1 Peter 1:3–4).

This inheritance is better than any 401(k) that one can have in this world! With this inheritance, we need not worry about the ups and downs of worldly investments. Our inheritance is being kept safe and secure in heaven for us.

SO WHAT ABOUT YOU?

I love talking to other believers about our faith, sharing the promises of God. I enjoy sharing and counseling the principles in this book. But I'm always aware that we must get beyond talking and teaching and reading, and focus on the *doing*.

So many of the parables of Jesus are about people who waited one day too long, workers who didn't get busy in the fields soon enough, or homeowners who weren't ready for the burglar. At some point we have to get up and do something.

"For the kingdom of God is not a matter of talk but of power" (1 Corinthians 4:20). You simply can't experience the power of God merely by talking about it. If talk were power, can you imagine how much of it we would generate in all our churches and Bible studies and Internet discussions each week? We'd solve the national energy question and other problems of the world overnight!

Why not give up your small ambitions?

My prayer is that, in reading this book, your soul has been stirred in several directions. The first, of course, is that you will have been motivated to seek a deeper fellowship with God. That's the wellspring for all that we're talking about.

Next, I hope you've found yourself thinking more deeply about your resources, particularly your possessions, and the meaning of them, than ever before. Why do you have them? What does God want you to do with them?

Then I hope you've become more conscious of eternal reality. I pray that you're far less prone to the terrible illusion that what we can see and hear and touch is all there is.

The eternal realities, the kingdom realities, are the ones that eventually define us.

Finally, I hope that you're making plans to organize your entire life as an investment in the kingdom of God—yourself, your relationships, your actions, your values, and your possessions. This may require a great deal of time. I would suggest taking devoted time, with your family if applicable, to work through the various changes you will need to make. Have a family retreat and discuss these things. How will your calendar reflect your kingdom priorities? What will your life look like when the changes are implemented?

Choose to be one of the strategic few who will make the greatest difference for the advancement of Christ's Kingdom.

Remember, it's not a matter of obligation, but of sheer joy. You're simply giving in to God's desire for you to be the person he designed you to be. You're saying yes to the great adventure he has plotted out for your life, and you'll never look back. I've never known a devoted believer with a kingdom mindset who decided to scale back to the world's values.

YOUR PERSONAL INVENTORY

All of us are "in process" and are "on the way" to eternity. As we practice soaking our heart in the Word of God, sowing to the Spirit, and flowing with the Spirit as he changes our attitudes and thinking, we will be transformed and consumed with the desire to want more of what the God of provision has for us. The following questions may help you discover changes God wants to bring about in your life through the power of his indwelling Spirit.

1. Am I sufficiently committed to the Word of God? What changes in my schedule do I need to make so that I can spend an appropriate amount of time in it? Who can I ask to hold me accountable to doing this? What specific daily reading plan will I use?

2. Am I sufficiently committed to spending time with God, soaking my mind and heart in his goodness? When will I do this every day? Where? Who can hold me accountable? What strategy for prayer will I use?

3. To what extent is greed an issue in my life? What is my relationship to money and possessions? Having come to some conclusions on those questions, what changes do I need to make? What are the action steps for making those changes?

4. Who's the "boss" in my life? If I'm completely honest, who or what is more important than any other consideration? If I don't like the answer, what will it take to change it? Who can help me with this?

5. Having reviewed the chapters describing kingdom attitudes and principles, which one is the biggest challenge for me? How will I trust God to direct my heart in that area? How will I know when I've changed? Who can pray with me about this?

6. What does my kingdom investment portfolio look like right now? How would Jesus evaluate my use of the resources that he has entrusted to me, if he were to return today? What obstacles are keeping me from being a more effective manager of what he has given me? How will I attack those obstacles?

7. What principles will guide me in the future as I look upon myself as a kingdom investor? How does God want me to begin? What's the plan? When will I start, who will I tell, and what will be my goals?

PRESS ON

None of us can look at where we've been and feel totally satisfied. Not one of us can think deeply about where we are without seeing the need for improvement.

This is no time for guilt, which only enhances negative feelings and a "can't do" attitude. Instead, trust God, whose tender mercies are new every morning. He is concerned with your future, not your past. Let's pay one more visit to Paul, in Roman house arrest as he writes that wonderful, joyful letter to his friends in Philippi. He speaks of the greatest goal of his life, to know Christ and experience his crucifixion and resurrection. Then he says:

> *Not that I have already obtained all this, or have already arrived at my goal, but I press on to take hold of that for which Christ Jesus took hold of me. Brothers and sisters, I do not consider myself yet to have taken hold of it. But one thing I do: Forgetting what is behind and straining toward what is ahead, I press on toward the goal to win the prize for which God has called me heavenward in Christ Jesus.*
>
> Philippians 3:12–14

As you consider the questions contained throughout this book, and you gaze at your investment plan, I hope you can look at it with hope rather than intimidation. "Not that I've already obtained all this," you can say with Paul, "but I'm *pressing on*."

Pressing on toward what? To take hold of the thing God has taken hold of you for.

God has a grip on you, my friend. And he wants you to get a grip on something, too: his mission for you. And as you do so, you will forget the past and simply start pushing for that prize for which God has called you toward the heavenly life, the life you experience in Christ.

That's what I call being *consumed* with a mission—consumed the way a crackling fire consumes a log; consumed the way a parched throat takes a drink of living water; consumed the way passionate people are, who live for one thing and one thing only.

> *My soul is consumed with longing for your laws at all times.*
>
> Psalm 119:20

Why not give up your small ambitions? Look around you. Everything you see will be gone someday. The Lord and his Word will remain, souls will remain, and the things you do and give for him today—they will remain, too. Regardless of where God has placed you or how many resources he has entrusted to you, choose to be one of the strategic few who will make the greatest difference for the advancement of Christ's Kingdom.

For me, the knowledge of that is enough to consume every moment of time I have left. This is what *KingdomNomics* is all about.

What about you?

APPENDIX A

YOU ARE WHAT YOU ATE

The message is clear! God's life and power become reality for those who diligently seek him and store up his Word in their hearts. I often use acrostics to help me remember important concepts and verses as I soak my mind in God's Word. ATE is one of these.

>   **A:** Accept and Assimilate God's Word in your heart. "Humbly accept the word planted in you, which can save you" (James 1:21).

>   **T:** Trust in it. "Commit your way to the LORD, Trust also in Him, And He shall bring it to pass" (Psalm 37:5, NKJV).

>   **E:** Expect God to work in your life. "For the eyes of the LORD run to and fro throughout the whole earth, to show Himself strong on behalf of those whose heart is loyal to Him" (2 Chronicles 16:9, NKJV).

APPENDIX B

BUTTON PUSHERS

God uses certain verses and passages from his Word to push my internal buttons. That creates inside me an intense desire to see the truth of certain passages become reality in my own life. I desire intensely—even crave—that God will reveal more of himself to me. I want him to make known his ways so that I may know him. I want him to speak to me as he did to Moses and others whose stories are in the Bible.

The Bible makes it clear that these truths can be and should be the desire of our heart. We need to meditate on these verses and assimilate them internally. They are our spiritual "M & Ms," verses that we want to *memorize* and *meditate* on.

I have a great many "button pushers," but here are a few of my favorites:

- Commit your way to the LORD; trust in him, and he will act. (Psalm 37:5, ESV)

- From of old no one has heard or perceived by the ear, no eye has seen a God besides you, who acts for those who wait for him. (Isaiah 64:4, ESV)

- "Call to Me, and I will answer you, and show you great and mighty things, which you do not know." (Jeremiah 33:3, NKJV)

- The LORD confides in those who fear him; he makes his covenant known to them. (Psalm 25:14, NIV84)

Appendix C

PERSONALIZING THE WORD

Newcomers to the Bible are often overwhelmed by the size of the book, by its many different writers and styles of literature, and by what seems to them to be obscure history and ancient culture. The key to getting past these fears, and enjoying the treasure of God's Word, is to *personalize* it and make it *operative* in our lives. Take a small passage, identify a few key words, and reflect on how it applies to you personally. Let's take a look at how we can do this by looking at a passage in the prophetic book of Jeremiah.

> *When your words came, I ate them;*
> *they were my joy and my heart's delight,*
> *for I bear your name, LORD God Almighty.*
> Jeremiah 15:16

Think for a moment about "eating" or "consuming" something. Most of us understand that a simple pill, such as aspirin, must be consumed and assimilated into our bodies or its healing power can't help us. Jeremiah said something similar about the holy words of Scripture: he "ate" them!

This means he memorized them, meditated upon them, and assimilated the Scriptures into his life. He took the scriptures from the parchment into his head, from there to his heart, where they were in position to impact his mind, will, emotions, and behavior.

Jeremiah had to search the Word of God. This is part of the process of assimilating it. There's a great difference between simply reading words, and meditating upon them until they become a part of who we are. When we fully fix our minds on God's Word, God's Spirit interacts with us—that happens with no other book in this world! He rewires us from the inside. He changes our attitudes and our values.

We read that God rewards those who *diligently* seek him. I must constantly ask myself if I'm doing that, and if I see in my life those rewards he promises to true seekers. *Diligently* means that as often and intentionally as possible, I bring these precious verses to mind and evaluate their meaning for me during that moment. I want my mind to be in sync with what is on God's mind, so that he can bring me into harmony with his plan.

Knowing that God rewards those who diligently seek him, I can be certain of something incredible: He is going to swing into action in my personal life as I recall these verses and pursue their implications. How does that affect me? It fills me with anticipation for God's mighty workings in the world I inhabit. This is how Jeremiah thought, and it's how you and I need to think as well.

Later in Jeremiah we find him quoting God: "Call to Me, and I will answer you, and show you great and mighty things, which you do not know" (Jeremiah 33:3, NKJV). Someone once referred to this verse as "God's telephone number." Just imagine–call to him! This verse is one that

I keep close to my heart, as others would remember 9-1-1 or the phone number of the one person in all the world who is closest to them. This is a promise that I can call upon the Creator of this universe, and be answered—and then be shown amazing things. Just thinking about that promise changes me, raising my anticipation of the workings of God. That verse, then, is a major *button pusher.* (See Appendix B.) God uses it to push my inner buttons all the time!

I'm reminded once again that what God did for Moses and Abraham and David, he will do for all of us. God showed them mighty things they did not know, and he is eager to do the same for you and for me. Why shouldn't I take him up on that promise? Why shouldn't you?

I'm greedy—in the best sense—for the wonders God wants to show me. I crave them every single day, and that craving energizes my life and my goals.

God has designed our hearts and minds in accordance with the works he has for us to accomplish. He tells us he will answer when we call, he will live within us, and he will act to fulfill his promises. These ideas amaze and humble me, and they also provide a deep incentive for me to know his promises.

As we believe and act on these promises, the Word becomes operative in us.

APPENDIX D

TEN PRINCIPLES FOR OUR FAMILY FOUNDATION

I n my family, we've set up a foundation that allows us to help finance Christian projects in line with the Great Commission, Christian education, and healthcare, all administered in the name of Jesus Christ. Most families, I realize, do their giving on a much less formal or organized basis. However, we came to the belief that we should be just as deliberate and intentional about what we give as we are about what we earn. After all, this is our investment in eternity. It's our venture designed to last forever. Why be overly casual about it?

Let me share with you some of the principles that guide the way we make decisions and minister together in our family group. I don't necessarily suggest these should be your guidelines, but they've worked for us and they may be helpful to your family as you make your plans.

Our intention is to make as much as we can, save as much as we can, and give as much as we can. We don't establish a fixed percentage for our gift, because for us, this feels a bit legalistic. While we're organized, we also want to give spontaneously from the heart. Giving *cheerfully* is extremely important to us.

We honor those who tithe, but we don't limit ourselves in that way. We have an "open hands" policy, depending on the project before us and our holdings at the moment. We know neither is a coincidence, and ask God what he wants us to do. For the most part, we limit our giving to organizations with whom we've established long-term relationships over the years.

We maintain a "base floor" for the foundation's capital requirements. We remember that seed capital is always needed to generate more wealth if the financial environment permits. Future giving depends upon this balance.

God's Word endures forever, and so do people. Therefore, the Great Commission guides all our giving; when we invest in sharing the gospel with people, we are making eternal investments.

We engage in further financial planning so we can take advantage of future opportunities for giving that may arise.

We are careful to do nothing that might interfere with our ability to give as the Lord leads us to give at maximum levels of generosity, goodness, good works, sharing, and sowing bountifully.

We will be cheerful givers using the "reasonable standard" mentioned in Romans 12:1 (offering all that we are as "living sacrifices," pleasing to God). Our key giving passages: 2 Corinthians 9; 1 Timothy 6:17-19; Luke16:1-13; 19:1-14.

We give while we live. We constantly ask, "Is there a good reason this gift shouldn't be given immediately?"

We do what we can to pass on these values to the next generation. Every boat leaves a wake behind it; so does every life. So we want to be givers not just of money but of ideas and Christian values.

We look for "wow" investments—those opportunities that make us say, "We *have* to have a piece of that!" Certain projects seem to call out to us, just like certain secular investments do as we diversify. I love exciting investments in God's eternal kingdom.

ENDNOTES

[1] http://biblicalstewardship.net/statistical-research-on-stewardship. Accessed February 26, 2013.

[2] C. S. Lewis, *Mere Christianity* (New York: MacMillan, 1966), 118.

[3] Statistics taken from http://www.generousgiving.org. Accessed December 4, 2012.

[4] George Barna, ed., *Leaders on Leadership: Wisdom, Advice, and Encouragement on the Art of Leading God's People* (Ventura, CA: Gospel Light, 1988), 102.

[5] Nicholas D. Kristof, "Evangelicals Without Blowhards," *The New York Times,* July 30, 2011.

[6] http://www.pewforum.org/christian/global-christianity-exec.aspx. Accessed October 28, 2012.

[7] Ben Patterson, *The Grand Essentials* (Nashville, TN: Word, 1988), 63.

CPSIA information can be obtained at www.ICGtesting.com
Printed in the USA
LVOW071737020713

340945LV00001BA/1/P